TEACHER
ON THE RUN
True Tales of Classroom Chaos

TEACHER ON THE RUN

True Tales of Classroom Chaos

FRANCIS GILBERT

✳ SHORT BOOKS

First published in 2005 by
Short Books
3A Exmouth House, Pine Street
London EC1R OJH

This paperback edition published in 2006
10 9 8 7 6 5 4 3 2

A CIP catalogue record for this book
is available from the British Library.

ISBN 1-904977-55-3

Printed in Great Britain by
Bookmarque Ltd, Croydon, Surrey

All the characters, except for myself and Michael Donaghy, are entirely fictional, people of my imagination, while the incidents are based on real events.

To Ellen and Arthur Wagner

PART ONE

PARADISE GAINED

The moment I stepped outside the Tube station, I caught the familiar scents and sounds of the High Street: the smell of fried noodles from the Chinese takeway, the swish of the branches of the oak trees fringing the "village" green, and the airy perfumes wafting about the immaculately tended front gardens of the detached houses. Even the texture of the clean pavement that wound down to the school felt like I was treading on my own memories.

I was back. I was back and I was glad to be back. I had never thought that I would say this, but it was true. I was grateful to be home. This polite London suburb was where I had grown up and from where I had tried so hard to escape. But my loathing towards it had changed so radically now that I felt joyously happy to be enfolded in its embrace.

I dusted down my smart clothes in the windscreen of a new BMW, took a deep breath and headed down the hill. I was very different from the hippy scruff-bag I used to be: the long, greasy hair had been clipped and washed, the Paisley shirts had been chucked out and replaced by respectable ones from a mail order catalogue, the dirty jeans and corduroys had vanished and now I always wore a suit and tie. I was a new me.

The ch-ch-ch-changes had truly happened. I had been teaching in Tower Hamlets for the past few years in one of the toughest comprehensives in the country. It had been bottom of the school league tables. In it, I had passed my probationary year as a teacher but I had encountered some very unruly classes and, while I had learnt a lot there, I had been desperate to get out.

I had been a different person when I started out in teaching. A socialist who believed that education could transform the lives of poverty-stricken children. But years of encountering intractable social problems, and feeling like I had made little impact in the classroom, had changed my views. There had been moments when I felt I would be forced to spend the rest of my working life teaching classes where *Macbeth* had to be reduced to three lines and every lesson had to have a fill-in-the-blanks worksheet. I reflected that I had been teaching at such a low level that I hadn't actually been teaching at all, more just keeping control of classes.

To many people, this new school, Humbards, was just another 'bog standard' comprehensive. To me – someone who had felt he had been trapped in a nightmare – it was heaven. Its average results and average kids represented the crème de la crème in my eyes. This was going to be my first day as a *proper* teacher. If only I had known then how things would turn out – how much more complex one's experience is than it may at first seem. With time I would realise that perhaps my contribution in Tower Hamlets had not been so futile after all.

***

As I descended the hill, I observed the children who were making their way towards the school gates and reflected that none of them appeared to be fighting, smoking, running out into oncoming traffic, throwing things at passing cars or spitting into the gutter. Their faces seemed calm and happy, their bodies well nourished and orderly, their uniforms clean and correct.

Had I looked like them when I was a pupil at the school? With a pang, I remembered my over-sized uniform and my anxiety. Why had I been so anxious? None of these children looked particularly worried about life, but I definitely had been. The memory of my anxiety was so deeply written into my brain that I could feel it now, surging through me for no good reason. I certainly wasn't worried about *teaching* at the school. That was going to be a doddle. So why this sudden panic attack? I had actually been a pupil at this school for just a few months before my parents moved me to the local public school down the road. A shy and nervous eleven-year old – were those days still so very close?

I took some more deep breaths and entered the precincts of the school. It was just as I remembered it. The delightful, tree-lined quad, the vast, wooden panelled dining room, the modern, brightly-lit science block, the colourful art department, the huge gymnasium, the playing field and the large playgrounds. It was a big, well-resourced school that had enough trees and flowers to make it seem welcoming.

A CLASSROOM OF ONE'S OWN

I checked in at the main office, where I was told to go to the English department. After ascending some stairs, I found my classroom, which I had been shown on my interview day. Oh, to have my very own classroom, what bliss! It was massive and it overlooked the quad. I could almost imagine I was teaching at Cambridge University, such was the luxury of my surroundings compared with where I had come from. I even had my own filing cabinet and cupboard! I would be able to file all the pupils' work and stow expensive equipment away.

I unpacked all the clobber from my rucksack and set about re-arranging my room. I had been preparing for this first week for about three months – ever since I learnt that I had got the job. Because I had visited the school the previous term, I was fully armed with worksheets and a register of pupils' names. I looked at my timetable again. I still couldn't believe it. Instead of being given lots of lower school classes to teach, I was teaching A-Level English Literature, GCSE Literature and Language, and a nice selection of lower school classes. In my previous school, you couldn't teach A-Level – there was no sixth form – and only the most senior teachers got to teach the prestigious GCSE courses.

IT'S MY EARS, OLD CHAP

A face shimmered at the window of my classroom. It belonged to a stooped but smiling figure, in a large blue shabby suit, with big glasses and a deaf-aid in one ear. I remembered Mr Morgan, but he didn't remember me. More than fifteen years before, I'd sat in the back of his English class as he'd railed in his booming voice about the barbarism of clichés. At eleven I didn't know what a cliché was but I quickly learned; he was an eccentric but fascinating teacher. He'd been much, much fatter then, but he'd always worn the deaf-aid.

"You see, it's my hearing old chap, I can't actually hear

the bally students reading out Thomas Hardy's poetry. With novels and such like it's easy because I insist that they read silently and then test 'em. But poetry has to be read aloud to do it any justice and so I just feel I can't teach it," he said. He pressed his finger to his deaf-aid and then twiddled something that was inside the jacket pocket of his dusty blue suit.

I suddenly remembered. Mr Morgan's deafness had meant he'd missed much of the pupils' banter about him. When pupils mouthed words in silence he'd thought they were talking to him. Conversely they'd been able to say some very rude things to him with a smile on their faces and he'd nodded graciously. I wondered whether they were still doing it.

I gulped at the memory. "Yes, of course, I'll teach Thomas Hardy's poetry."

I didn't have much knowledge about Hardy's poetry at the time but that didn't matter. I was absurdly and ridiculously happy. I felt like a prisoner from Colditz who had escaped and found a job in toytown. I was a hard-bitten LA cop who had landed a job solving a murder with Miss Marple. I was a heavy-weight boxer who had been asked to fight in the featherweight division. I was in dreamland.

Mr Morgan only added to the air of genteel unreality as he said, "Now old bean, I must show you around the school. You'll get terribly lost here. I do find that teachers like you get quite lost here."

His manner, which I remembered as having been intimidating and loud when I was a child, seemed almost comic now. Perhaps it was because he had lost so much weight and seemed like a skinny ghost of the great balloon he used to be, or perhaps it was because of the way he peered so deeply and closely at you when you were talking to him, constantly adjusting his hearing aid.

"What do you mean?"

Mr Morgan gave a knowing cackle. He spread three fingers in the air. I had another memory of him doing this in the classroom; all problems – literature and just about the whole of life – were divided up into threes for him.

"There are three components to your getting lost here. Firstly, there is the physical layout of the school, which is, I have to say, rather confusing. I have frequently found young teachers wandering around in a daze not being able to get to their classrooms. But I daresay, you will not suffer from this, as you have your own classroom.

"Secondly, there are the pupils. Always a problem in a school. They are lost and they will lose you if you are not careful.

"I remember teaching here twenty years ago. Oh, how different things were then! The pupils actually knew how to behave and to work!"

THE THIRD WOMAN

Mr Morgan tailed off as we entered the staffroom. I wanted to ask what the third component was but all the staff seemed to be assembling for a meeting. I scanned them. They looked like typical teachers: the men were in suits ranging from the shabby to the reasonably smart, the women seemed mostly middle-aged, although I could see that there were quite a few young attractive ones as well. What a contrast from my previous school! There were no punk haircuts, no men in earrings, no teachers who looked like tramps here. I was back in a place called normality.

The Headteacher, Mr Woodham, stood up and the staff immediately fell silent. He smiled cheerfully and said that he hoped everyone had had a good holiday. Then he introduced a couple of members of new staff, including me. I stood up as he mentioned my name. Sixty pairs of eyes swivelled round to look at me. People laughed appreciatively when Woodham explained that I had come to rescue the English Department. But I could see Mrs Lee, my Head of Department, squirming in her seat. It wasn't a joke that she appreciated at all.

Mr Morgan leaned over and whispered as he pointed surreptitiously at the frowning Head of English, "That, old-chap, is the third component. The third woman, you might say!"

MRS LEE

Mrs Lee bustled up to me after the meeting. She was a vigorous, sharp-eyed woman in her late fifties who reminded me somewhat of my impressive grandmother. She wore a long, grey skirt, a no-nonsense grey cardigan and a cream-white blouse. Her hair was grey and curly, and topped her head like a crown. I remembered that she had looked exactly the same when I had been a pupil nearly fifteen years ago; she had seemed quite frightening then, but she exuded an impatient camaraderie now.

"Ah Francis, just the person we need; someone who looks healthy! The poor boy who was here before was on drugs, and was, alas, just not suitable. Lasted a day. Never advisable to be consuming narcotics in large quantities in the teaching profession. I don't recommend it," she said without a trace of irony. Taking my arm, she guided me to the room where I was supposed to register my tutor group – a different room from my actual teaching room. I wasn't that shocked by this sudden and unexpected tactile gesture because I had encountered it in my previous school; the secretary there had had a similarly "mumsy" air about her. In fact, I found it immensely comforting. Mrs Lee had already humanised the place for me.

Mrs Lee left me at the top of the stairs with the words, "I think you'll find everything running like a smoothly oiled, precision machine here." She winked and swung her huge handbag, which had papers poking out of it, in the direction of the English Department. As I walked to my tutor group, I thought about her words. Where had I heard them before?

It was just as I was entering the corridor that housed my tutor group that I realised: she was quoting from Captain Mainwaring in *Dad's Army*!

I didn't have time to think much about her tone because I now had to deal with my new Year 8 tutor group. I was greeted by the Head of Year with a cheery chuckle. Again, I remembered him – but he clearly didn't know me – as a superb PE teacher who had encouraged me to be a fly-half at rugby. Yes, Jim Saunders was a great teacher. He looked quite a bit older: his ginger hair was sprinkled with grey and his skin was leathery and red. But his bluff, hearty manner was exactly the same.

"Ah, so, Mr Gilbert, you've come along to join the Year 8 scrum!" he proclaimed. He shook my hand with real warmth, and handed me my register, and a folder containing all the necessary details of the tutor group. And then with a wink, he said, "Any trouble, send the blighters to my office. But you've been in Tower Hamlets, haven't you? You shouldn't have many problems!"

Everything in this school was so different from my last. The teachers seemed genuinely merry; the atmosphere felt neither violent nor hideously deprived.

***

I wiped the smile off my face as I entered my tutor room. The twelve-year-olds were chatting at their desks as I arrived. It was a music room and the outer edges of it were covered with keyboards and computers. Miraculously, not one pupil was playing with the keyboards.

I took a deep breath, raised my head to the ceiling and stared at the class, waiting for them to be silent. A few caught on straight away and asked their mates to turn round and listen. Within seconds, the whole class was silent and gazing at me with wide eyes and rosy cheeks. I maintained my stern face, but inwardly I was yelling for joy. I had never seen anything like this before. In my previous school, I could have stood for the whole of the tutor session – twenty minutes – and none of them would have been silent.

Only one boy persisted in whispering to the person sitting next to him. I knew that I had to hit him hard (so to speak).[1]

"Right, you there! Stand up now!" I shouted. The whole class sat bolt upright in their seats. I thought about asking him his name, but then remembered from my last school that asking such a question at this point was fatal. Often kids supplied the wrong name making me look like a total idiot until I found out their real one.

The boy stood up. He was quite a fat boy, with plump, freckled cheeks. He was one of the few whose uniform was not very smart.

"Why isn't your top button done up? Tuck your shirt in! I only want the smartest pupils in this tutor group, because I intend to make this tutor group the smartest one in the school."

I watched as the boy scrabbled to tuck in his shirt and do up his tie. I could tell immediately that this boy was winnable because of the way he responded to my commands. There was no smirking, no reluctance to tidy up his uniform, no surliness.

"Sit down. Any more talking when I am talking, and you'll get a detention," I said.

---

[1] Pre-emptive strikes. The Italian Renaissance philosopher Machiavelli wrote the best teacher training guide, *The Prince*, in 1515. One of the most important pieces of advice he gives in the book is this: "In seizing a state, the usurper [a teacher taking over a new class] ought to examine closely into all those injuries which it is necessary for him to inflict, and to do them all at one stroke so as not to have to repeat them daily [always hand out detentions to trouble-makers during the honeymoon period of the first few weeks, and not lots of them months afterwards]; and thus by not unsettling men he will be able to reassure them [appear tough to begin with], and win them to himself with benefits [praise should be handed out to the well-behaved]. He who does otherwise, either from timidity or evil advice, is always compelled to keep the knife in his hand; neither can he rely on his subjects, nor can they attach themselves to him, owing to their continued and repeated wrongs [if you don't strike first, you'll always be dogged by disobedience and have to punish the students far too often]. For injuries ought to be done all at one time, so that, being tasted less, they offend less; benefits ought to be given little by little, so that the flavour of them may last longer [hand out merits regularly and not in one splurge].

The boy sat down with a crest-fallen face, and I even felt a little sorry for him. I knew that I had genuinely frightened him. Having spent nearly three years in one of the roughest schools in the country, I had acquired a slightly psychotic air.

Now that I had every pupil's rapt attention, I introduced myself: "I am Mr Gilbert, your new form tutor. I know that you are Year 8 now. You have been in the school a year, and you probably think that you know the place. You will know it better than me, and so I am expecting you to help me out. But I am also expecting you to BEHAVE. When you are in my tutor group, you LISTEN to every word I say. The register is a LEGAL document, and I am obliged by law to make sure that you are here or absent. I expect everyone to come to school UNLESS THEY ARE HALF-DEAD! I won't have excuses about having colds, or even flu. You come in. Every piece of research shows that it is your attendance which will have the biggest influence upon the results you get in the end. If you don't turn up, how can you learn?

"There are also a few other rules I would like to spell out to you. You wear the correct uniform. Why is it important to wear the proper uniform?"

A girl stuck her hand up immediately. "Because it symbolises one's commitment to the school. The school's values are implicitly enshrined in the uniform; the uniform represents equality of opportunity."

I gulped. I couldn't believe that a twelve-year-old was talking like this. Sensing that I was amazed by her complex answer, she added: "We did it as a project last year, sir."

I continued to question the class about why they shouldn't bring Walkmans, jewellery or money into school – this was the pre-mobile phone era – and why they should not chew gum and so on. Everyone put their hands up, and answered my questions. Even the fat boy with freckles did.

I then took the register, working out that the slightly naughty boy was called Billy Johns, and the incredibly bright girl was Melissa Cruickshank. I scanned some of the paperwork that Jimmy Saunders had given me. Every child in the class had two married parents except for Billy Johns, who appeared to be living with a relative who didn't have his name. Only three pupils were on free school meals.

Again, I marvelled at how different it all was from my last school, where I had had a tutor group in which virtually everyone was on free school meals! Added to which, over three-quarters of my class in Tower Hamlets had come from broken homes, and lived with single parents.

At the end of the tutor session, I praised the class: "I've heard you are a brilliant class, and I can see that now. I know you are going to be perfectly well-behaved for me, and that you are going to have a good time."

Just as I was finishing what I was saying, I noticed Billy

Johns whispering to his neighbour again. I pounced immediately. "Right Billy Johns, detention with me after school today for talking while I am talking. See me here at 3.30pm."

I could see that he wanted to protest. He was just about to open his mouth and say that he wasn't talking but I anticipated him. "There's no arguing with me in this class, otherwise you get a longer detention. My word is law. That is that. Right then, Year 8 stand behind your chairs. Quietest people go first!"

I dismissed the class row by row, watching them with folded arms. They all filed out in silence. Wow! Behaving like a psycho really worked! Or did it?

CLASSES BEGIN

This first day was going to be vital. If I looked like an idiot today then I would spend weeks, perhaps months, trying to recover the authority I had lost.

My first class was Year 7, eleven-year-olds. I was waiting for them outside my classroom like a sheriff standing guard before the court-house. I could tell by the slightly cheeky, smiley expressions on their faces that these little boys and girls thought they knew the school better than me. After all, they have been in the school a whole term longer.

I watched them calmly as they giggled and simpered in a

long line outside my classroom. MY classroom. I said the words to myself and smiled. I still couldn't believe that I had this enormous room to myself! I had never had such luxuries in teaching before.

"I'm waiting," I said quietly. Most of them started listening – a few smirks melted into looks of concern – but there was a rump of rowdiness at the end of the line. I walked up there and stared. AND STARED. I didn't have to say anymore because the children stopped talking. I smiled, a nasty, sharp-toothed grin that I reserved for predators. The kids could already feel my confidence. They sensed that I was no nervous rookie.

"Now I expect all of you to go into the class and sit down quietly in REGISTER order. I am going to insist upon boys sitting next to girls."

There was a little, generic sigh of resentment at this news but no real discontentment. I had become a connoisseur, during my years in Tower Hamlets, at judging the unruliness of a class by the noises it makes.

At the lowest end of the scale there was this sort of class; young, biddable, winnable children who could be easily frightened with a correctly placed shout or admonition.

This breed of class tended to bubble like a mountain spring with excitement when they were enjoying the work, or drizzle very quietly like summer rain when they were feeling hard-done-by.

At the other end of the spectrum, there were volcanic classes who were constantly rumbling and surging with noise, frequently erupting with great geysers of molten sound, and once every so often exploding in great fiery wreaths of violence and contempt.

For someone who had endured the mayhem of volcanic classes, I found myself loving the little sprinkle of sound that this Year 7 emitted. Nevertheless I was determined to impose silence if I needed it. While I was taking the register, I noticed a girl whispering to her partner.

"Stand up immediately! How dare you spoil my taking the register!" I shouted. It was the first time that I had let rip the full splendour of my Tower-Hamlets trained voice and I could see a number of pupils reeling from the shock.

The girl stood up, quivering. I let her stand there for a while, and continued with the register. She put her hand up meekly at the end.

"Please sir, I'm really sorry," she said, tears edging out of her eyes.

"OK, sit down," I said.

I marvelled at the effect that I had had upon the girl. She was frightened of me. And judging from the anxious eyes that were scanning her and me, the rest of the class were frightened too. It was great; I had that trusty old friend, fear, on my side. I had spent most of my time in my last school being frightened of my classes in various degrees but now everything was reversed; I was inspiring a great deal more fear than I felt. What luxury!

I handed out my introductory poem to the class. It was an acrostic poem, which spelt my name and the rules I expected the pupils to obey. I wouldn't have dared dish out such a document to my Tower Hamlets' classes, but I had guessed that the children would be more receptive here. I had spent quite a bit of time composing it during the holidays. It went like this:

Minds are like gardens: they must be tended;
Reading is sunlight for the plants.

Good manners help everyone.
Independence of mind is vital to success.
Listen like a mouse, watch like a hawk.
Believe in yourself and take pride in your work.
Early planning, fluent writing and careful editing are crucial.
Respect your teacher, your environment, and yourselves.
Try hard and you will enjoy yourself!

I asked the class to read through the poem in pairs and write down five questions to ask about it. They carried out this task quickly, and soon I was gazing at a forest of hands poking and jolting up in the air, begging me to ask them to read out their questions.

"Why are minds like gardens? I thought I had a brain, not a garden," Henry, a boy with a great mane of blond hair and blue eyes, asked. He stared at me with real sincerity; he wasn't taking the piss. I threw his question to the rest of the class.

"You need to tend to your brain. You have to read to make it grow," Sheila said. She was a very serious-looking creature with pale skin, sunken eyes, and long, lank black hair. She was obviously very impatient with silly little boys. Far too sophisticated for them.

"Tend to your hair," I heard Samantha whisper under her breath.

I pounced immediately. "I won't have that! I won't have anyone make critical remarks of anyone in this class! How dare you! Stand up now!"

Samantha, who was a skinny girl with buck-teeth and spots on her nose, shambled to her feet, with her head bowed. "Sorry sir," she said.

"You shouldn't be apologizing to me, you should be saying sorry to Henry," I said.

She turned to the remarkably blond Henry and uttered a miserable sorry. I thanked her and said she could sit down.

I then asked one member of the pair who had devised the questions to go and put those questions to another person sitting in front of them, who would attempt to provide the answers. This involved a bit of shuffling around and would have resulted in chaos with a difficult class, who would have seen it as an excuse to wander around the room and not do any work. But these anxious little sparks flittered with excitement and rushed to ask their questions.

"Right, you have ten minutes in which to answer the questions!" I said.

I wandered down the aisles of the classroom, listening to the children chatter about what it meant to be independent of mind, to carefully edit, to respect the environment and to enjoy yourself. As the winter sun shone at the windows, the dark branches of an ancient, tall yew tree stroked the glass. Down below, beyond the precincts of the school, suburban gardens nestled in the frosty light. It was cold outside, but inside it was warm and snug.

"Right, I'll count to three and I expect silence! 1,2,3!" I said loudly. Everyone was silent and eager to report back. Using the children's comments, I drew a spider diagram on the board of what the class thought the poem meant, and in the process, we agreed on the rules for my classroom. In particular, I emphasized the concept of 'respect' and tried to make the children see that there was a cogent reason for each of the rules. But they had twigged this.

I then asked them to write their own acrostic poem using

their own names. Some of them found this a bit difficult but most were able to come up with some decent efforts. Henry's poem went like this:

Henry, Henry is my name
Everyone calls me Hal
No one wants to call me Henry
Right now though
You can call me Henry.

It was not exactly the most revealing poem, but I kind of liked it, and he seemed particularly pleased with his efforts. I could see that he was someone who struggled to write at length, and I realised that this poem was quite an achievement for him. I praised him, and he read it out proudly to the class.

They all clapped when he finished. I was struck by the class's ability to co-operate and celebrate other pupils' successes. I had never come across a class before that had spontaneously clapped at one pupil's work. I recalled how I had had to guide pupils to applaud other people's work in my previous school in Tower Hamlets.

At the end of the lesson, I set the homework – which was to write a letter about themselves – and barked in my most military voice for the children to stand behind their chairs, and wait for me to dismiss them by name. I did this using the register, praising them again as I went. As I watched them disappear down the corridor, I thought they were going to be an exciting class to teach. All of them appeared to be literate, some of them seemed to be very intelligent, and only a few needed significant attention with their writing.

SEATING ARRANGEMENTS

My next class, Year 8, was a little more lively. As they lined up, I tried my staring trick with a group of giggling girls at the back of the queue but this didn't work. The girls, who seemed to be jumble of blond and brown hair because they were strangely entwined with each other, their arms all interlinked, just giggled more. I took a deep breath. I couldn't expect everything to be easy.

I frowned, and shouted, "Excuse me, but I think you are being extremely rude. I am your teacher and I expect you to line up quietly for my class!"

This had the desired effect. The girls disentangled themselves from each other, pulled long faces, and stood to attention. My voice ricocheted down the corridor, quietening down the rest of the queue as well. I walked to the front of the line and ushered them into my 'castle' – I was already beginning to think of my classroom as my heartland, my domain of which I was lord. I remembered a teacher in my previous school, Sean Carson, who had turned his classroom into a sort of pedagogical fortress, armed against every conceivable attack that the enemy – disruptive children – could mount against it. Of course, it was purely a psychological fortress – an embodiment of his educational mind – but its clean, immaculately presented environment appeared to induce a sort of awed reverence among the pupils.

I was determined that I would do the same with my classroom. Once again, I asked the pupils to sit boy next to girl, and in register order. There were quite a few complaints about this – a little surge of moaning swept through the class: "Oh what did he have to do that for?"

In particular, there was a boy who sat with folded arms at his desk, saying to his mate: "I ain't sitting next to no girl."

This class was going to be trickier than the last one. I called the kids to attention and explained that I would read out the names in the register and tell everyone where to sit.

"I reserve the right to sit you wherever I want you to sit. This classroom is MY castle, YOU obey me here, and there will be NO complaints."

My voice was determined, tinged with anger and aggression. It was noisy as I called out the names in the register. I would point with a very decisive finger at where I wanted the children to sit. Sometimes, I didn't exactly have them in register order and I could have hesitated, hummed and hawed about where to sit the selected pupil, but I opted for real decisiveness, whipping my hand at a desk and telling them to sit there.

I came to a boy whose name was Karl Jefferson. He was going to sit next to a mousey-haired girl with big glasses, and a hunched, shy stoop. The last person he wanted to sit next to. I could see that he was wearing a gold bracelet, and gold "gangsta-style" necklace. He also had that giveaway fat, insignia ring. I knew from my previous school that this was a sure sign that a pupil was fighting regularly. That kind of ring is a fantastic weapon, drawing blood when punched into the flesh with force.

I instructed him to sit in the alloted seat. He remained in his original seat. I knew that if I repeated my request again I would lose face; it would quite clearly prove that he was not following my instructions. So I walked over to the chair where he was supposed to be sitting, and said, "Is that school uniform you're wearing? I'm not sure that it is, is it?" I tapped the back of the chair as I said this.

This comment got him out of his chair. By changing the topic, I had managed to allow him to save face.

"Course, it's uniform. This," he said, holding up his ring to the light, 'is the most important piece of uniform I got!"

He "bowled" over to his new seat, grinning at the class while he brandished his ring.

34

"Oh," I said, with a gracious smile. "Perhaps, I'll investigate that later."

I'd achieved my objective, I'd managed to get Karl to sit next to a girl!

***

I gave out the acrostic poem again, and asked the class to do the same exercise. Instead of getting kids to work in pairs, I asked them to work individually, and read their questions about the poem to the person sitting next to them. They were very responsive, and listened in silence as I ran through my classroom rules with them.

I emphasised that they were to listen in silence to everything I said, and that they should always sit where I required them to sit. As with the previous class, I didn't mention punishments except to say that if they didn't do the work they were punishing themselves.

The giggling girls came up with the best poems. There was Julie, Kate and Sharmeen. Julie's acrostic was memorable, if flawed:

Jokes make
U feel
Lovely

35

In your
Ears

She broke out into more giggles as she passed it back to Kate, her friend, who was sitting behind her. She tried to stop me from seeing it, but I grabbed it before she could write her official version.

"Needs work," I said.

THE RED PUSTULE

Year 9 were entirely different. Puberty had distorted the boys' faces and bodies into weird shapes: long, slightly hairy chins, angular cheek bones, spotty cheeks, gangly arms and clumsy legs. They tussled with each other, making quite a noise as they lined up outside the classroom. I bounded outside, slamming the door behind me. The glass reverberated in its frame, and a few of the kids fell silent.

"Oi, you nearly broke that window mate," a boy with short-cropped ginger hair and pustular spots commented.

"I'm waiting for the class to be quiet," I said to him.

"Looks like you're going to wait for quite a while," he said, grinning at me and revealing a large hunk of metal wire encasing his teeth.

I took his advice. The last thing I wanted to do was have

36

this rowdy class – thirty largish adolescents – kicking their shoes against the corridor for the next twenty minutes, while I vainly waited for them to shut up. So I ushered them in. However, once inside the classroom, I did instruct them to sit in alphabetical order.

The uproar was intense. "What's the matter with you? You got psychological problems? You need your head examined!" the red-headed pustule with the braces said to me, while pointing at his head with a jabbing finger, mimicking a gesture that flashy rap stars did. I wasn't used to this kind of articulate insurrection and simply asked him to sit in the seat I'd asked him to.

The alphabet appeared to have placed him next to his mate, Albert Tench: a tall, thin-faced, long-necked character who reminded me of a Giacometti sculpture. Tench wouldn't have looked out of place in a museum next to the famous sculptor's *Head of a Man on a Rod* with his attenuated neck, shrunken cheeks and wide eyes. However, Tench was more verbal than his sculptural counterpart and irritated me intensely as he talked to the Red Pustule – as I already thought of him – while I was calling out the register. I knew I had to confront them.

"Excuse me, but I'm trying to teach a lesson here and you are supposed to be listening," I said with real force.

This shut up most of the class. All eyes swivelled to Will Jenkins, the red-headed pustule, and the Giacometti-necked

Trevor Tench. Will Jenkins just sniggered.

"It's the register, it ain't important. Chill out, guy. I thought you looked cool, but you're a nerd."

My response was immediate. I'd had enough of this kind of insolence in my previous school and I wasn't going to endure it here. I stood up, and pointed at the door: "Get out of my classroom now, and report to On Call." I had mugged up on the school procedures and was pleased to see that someone had instituted this disciplinary procedure; if a pupil misbehaved they could be sent to the dining hall where a senior member of staff would supervise them while they did their work. There had been a similar system in my previous school in Tower Hamlets but it was a disaster because the venue for On Call changed every lesson and no pupil knew quite where to go. Here, I could immediately see it worked because there was just one venue to send miscreants to.

Jenkins sighed, and leaned back in his chair. "Nah, you don't mean that, do ya? What have I done?"

"You have just been very rude to me, and I won't tolerate rudeness," I said.

Jenkins winked at his mate. "Have I been rude to him?"

"He didn't say anything," Tench said in a surprisingly deep voice.

"I think you could say I was being victimised," Jenkins added, peering around at the class looking for support. A few kids were grinning but I could sense that most of the class were sick of Jenkins. After all, they knew him far better than me, having spent two years and a term with him.

"GET OUT!" I thundered. "NOW!"

Jenkins did a mock cringe. "What's the matter with you? You got psychological problems or what?"

"You've already cracked that joke. Now go," I said. "Or do I have to get another teacher to escort you out of the class?"

I walked to the door and held it open. Jenkins slowly arose from his seat and slouched out of the class. Once he was gone, I got on immediately with explaining my poem. I dispensed with all the niceties of having them think of five questions to ask about it; I needed to impose myself upon the class and was determined to do this by lecturing them while they were listening.

With Jenkins gone, they all listened. Sending him On Call had acted as a deterrent. However, I hadn't seen the last of him. He re-emerged half-way through my talk about class rules, and handed me a note.

"This boy does not have the relevant forms for On Call, and there is no work for him to get on with. Yours, Kelvin Hacker."

I made a snap judgement to sit Jenkins in the class rather than faff around with all the paperwork that was necessary to put him On Call. I placed him at the front of the class and continued with my talk. He listened quietly. I didn't ask the class to write a poem for me; that felt a bit too babyish for this lot. Instead, I asked them to write me a detailed letter about themselves, going through the ways in which to lay out a formal letter.

They got on with it in silence. I had won! And I was also intrigued to see that even the worst of them could write a few paragraphs albeit sometimes badly spelt and grammatically turgid. In my previous school, those strugglers would have been top of the class. Hurray! I didn't have to write fill-in-the-gaps sheets for every lesson.

GENTILITY

I was in a bit of a daze when I watched the last of my new Year 9 class wash out of my classroom. I locked the door – I had my own key! And I sauntered down the corridor, my head swimming with thoughts about my classes.

I left the main building and walked over the tarmac to the staffroom. Everything felt so civilised here. There were no kids slapping me on the back in mock gestures of friendliness, no cussing, no swearing, no fighting.

In the staffroom, things were similarly genteel. Mrs Lee was knitting as she chatted to another elderly-looking teacher. Now how long would Mrs Lee have lasted in my previous school, I said to myself, as I walked over to her corner – about five seconds? Mrs Lee patted the seat next to her, and instructed me to sit down.

"Now, now, then, how were the little scamps with you?" I grinned and said that everything was fine except that I had had to send out Will Jenkins out of the class. Mrs Lee cringed a little.

"Oh dear little Will, he is an absolute nuisance, isn't he?" she said, resuming her knitting. "I taught him in the first year. His mother is a Headmistress, you know. Of somewhere rough. In the East End. Where you hail from. He's very reluctant to accept any voice of authority. Moral authority. Once, I gave him a two hour detention. He just had to sit and watch me knit. Poor boy was bored out of his mind. I think he plays too many computer games. Can be very insolent."

Mrs Lee's conversation continued in this vein for quite a while, meandering in and out of the topic of Will Jenkins, her knitting, his mother being a Headmistress, the terrible trash on television. Her cadences became almost hypnotic after a while as her words clicked in time to her knitting needles. She wouldn't let me say anything. Her friend, Grace Malmesbury, the Head of Home Economics, was obviously used to Mrs Lee and would murmur her assent every now and then as she read the *Daily Mail*.

But, after ten minutes of unsuccessfully trying to speak to

her, I spotted another English teacher hovering by the pigeon holes.

"Sorry, but I've got to just ask Yolanda something," I said.

"Don't split your infinitives, my dear. Now off you go," Mrs Lee said, without looking up from her knitting.

Unfortunately, at that point in my career – even though I had studied Latin at school – I didn't know about the split infinitive rules for Standard English and so I didn't understand why I had been told off.[2] I scuttled over to Yolanda Williams, the only young, attractive female teacher in the department. She had long, flowing black hair, piercing eyes, high cheek bones and amazing creamy brown skin.

"Hi Francis, I see you escaped!" she whispered, nodding at the two knitting women in the far corner. She leant towards me and the opened cuffs of her red shirt brushed against my

[2] English teachers and grammar. I was taught English at school during a time when it was not fashionable for English teachers to drill the students in grammatical terminology. I learnt all my grammar in Latin lessons. I was certainly not encouraged to teach grammar explicitly during my teacher training; I was actually encouraged by one English tutor to dispense with the apostrophe altogether. He regarded it as entirely unnecessary, an an upper-class invention devised to subjugate the working classes. However, all of this was about to change with the introduction of the Literacy Strategy, which insists that pupils are taught grammar. Mrs Lee had been in teaching so long that her ideas were about to become trendy again. I have to say, though, that as living proof that one can pass numerous exams and degrees (three to my name) without knowing too much about grammar, I am not so sure about this return to old-fashioned values; in recent years, having been forced to teach the Literacy Strategy, I have become disillusioned by the overuse of grammatical terminology in lessons. I understand it all thoroughly now, but the children don't and learning it often hampers their progress because it stops them from becoming fluent writers.

hand. She was close enough for me to feel the warmth of her body. I blushed. After all, I was a married man, and shouldn't have been noticing such things.

"Are there any schemes of work in the department? I mean, I've got all the syllabuses and everything but I don't seem to have found any other paperwork," I said.

This was a disingenuous question. I knew full well that there were no schemes of work – Mrs Lee had told me that she didn't bother with that kind of bureaucracy – but I knew it was a chance to bond with Yolanda. Perhaps, she would complain, that as a relatively new teacher – she'd only been at the school a year – she hadn't felt very supported.

She tipped her eyes to the heavens. "Are there schemes of work, my arse! They don't exist here. I don't know what Ofsted are going to say when they inspect the department."

This was wonderful. I had someone to moan to![3] I strolled with Yolanda to the canteen and we complained about schools that just were not prepared for the modern world; these old guys and gals just didn't know what had hit them with the new National Curriculum and Ofsted, and so on.

As we sat down at the staff dinner bench with our borstal

---

[3] Moaning. I like moaning teachers because I am one myself. I think moaning is a vital psychological mechanism that enables you to carry on teaching. If you don't vent your frustrations and instead carry them around with you, you end up going mad.

trays of pasta and peas, we agreed that we would try and devise some schemes of work together. I also asked Yolanda about Kelvin Hacker, the teacher who had sent me the terse note via Will Jenkins. Yolanda leaned close to me and whispered, "He has issues."

"Issues? What about?"

"I can't say here. But watch this space. Something's going to happen to that man and it isn't going to be good. I have an intuition about it."

This was all very strange but I couldn't get anything more out of her. I was to learn that Yolanda had this rather mysterious side: she often made cryptic comments.

I bounced into afternoon registration even happier than I had been in the morning. The class were still terrified of me and cowered in silence as I used my deepest voice to register them. I reminded Billy Johns that he was to meet me for a detention after school, and strode purposely to my afternoon lessons.[4]

This was the lesson I was most looking forward to. A-Level English Literature. The ultimate reason why I had become a teacher!

---

[4] Lessons after lunch. These are famously the worst. Children's behaviour is far, far worse after they have consumed a bag of chips, a chocolate bar and a can of Coke – the average meal in your average comprehensive.

SIXTH FORM CLASS

Jemima Killen yawned and stretched, and took off her jumper. She was a big girl; the way her jeans bulged over the pitifully small-looking chair made me worried for her safety. The chair was creaky under her weight. It wasn't particularly that she was fat; she was just big. She was a sixth former and because sixth formers didn't have to wear uniform, they already looked somehow too grown-up and trendy for school. This thought was only further reinforced by the removal of her jumper. My eyes almost popped. The volume of Thomas Hardy's poems that was in my hands nearly fell to the floor. I just could not believe that she had the nerve to wear such a tight-fitting, low-cut T-shirt.

What was I going to do? I felt I could not discuss the finer points of Thomas Hardy's grief about the death of his wife with those on show. They mocked the poor, wrinkled poet's whingeings about grief. They were a complete distraction from the spiritual themes of the verse.

There were only two boys in this class: two laddish characters surrounded by a lot of very articulate, very assertive girls. Clearly, the only perk they enjoyed was that they could ogle Jemima's breasts. I saw their eyes slide off the page and dart furtive glances towards them.

What made matters much worse was that Jemima was a

very vocal member of the class and spoke with the utmost seriousness about the poetry.

"I think Hardy is actually not grief-stricken at all. I mean, if he truly loved his wife he would have told her while she was alive. It was a bit late when she was dead," she said, leaning back and gathering her dyed blond hair into a pony tail.

What could I say – "Put your jumper back on"? Perhaps Mrs Lee would have said, "Put them away my dear"... I opted not to look at her.

In the lower school, dealing with misbehaviour was relatively straightforward. A kid annoyed you, you shouted at them, gave them a detention, told them not to do it again. Here, with these young adults before me, the issue of discipline was more complex and psychological. You couldn't just tell these articulate, high-achieving girls to shut up when they chose to have a little gossip with their neighbours; you couldn't yell at them for not wearing the right uniform. Or could you?

Despite my embarrassment about Jemima's T-shirt, the lesson went well. The pupils read a couple of Hardy's poems in pairs, presented dramatic readings to the class, each offering their own interpretation of a particular theme in the poetry. I finished the lesson with them writing their notes up. They were quite chatty about this, and I wondered if I should bellow at them to write in silence – as I would have done with my other classes – but I decided against this. I wanted to be their friend.[5]

DETENTION

Billy Johns was waiting for me in a rather hang-dog fashion in the form tutor room. He looked up at me with a sulky lip, but conciliatory eyes, and said, "I'm sorry for talking sir. I won't do it again."

His apology melted my heart. I had been intending to get him to write lines for ten minutes, but I gave him a lecture about obeying his teacher instead, and dismissed him.

GOING HOME

As I walked home, back to the train station through salubrious streets, I reflected that I was going to love it at the school. My day had gone so well. I had never had such a successful day in my previous school, even when things *were* going

---

[5] <u>Teachers who want to be the pupils' friend.</u> This is an error because if a teacher is doing his job properly he can never, ever be a friend in the sense that a friend rarely, if ever, orders someone to do a specific task. Teachers are always doling out orders. They speak in imperatives. I have come across teachers who, in an attempt to be friendly, have constantly changed their orders in a desperate bid to please their "friends". This is fatal because pupils just say that they are bored with a task and demand another one. The teacher then provides another task – if he can think of one – and the same response soon occurs. Chaos ensues.

well. I had never seen so many kids who were articulate, organised and happy. It made me think that perhaps much of a secondary school teacher's work ought already to have been done at primary school, and that if a child didn't get a good education *then,* all was lost.

It also made me aware that a settled family background was important.

FOUR MONTHS LATER – MAY

Mr Morgan stumbled along the corridor and then stopped. He leant on his walking stick and appeared to be gasping for breath. It was early in the morning, eight o'clock, and there weren't many people around – pupils or teachers. I watched him for a second as he gazed through the window at the windswept playground. Outside, the spring sunlight was tussling with a few crisp packets, making them wink and blink with light.

Mr Morgan was sweating, and appeared unusually meditative. I hurried along towards him, wondering whether he was having a heart attack. He appeared almost to be on the verge of tears.

"Are you all right Eustace?" I asked.

He jerked out of his reverie, and scrutinised me.

"Ah yes, Francis old chap, just a bit of a gippy tummy,

you know, nothing serious," he said.

With this, he left me, turned on his heels and poked his walking stick at the door to his office, which was slightly ajar. As he opened it, I saw that it was in a terrible mess: full of walking boots, wellingtons, old coats; maps were strewn everywhere, and so many papers littered his desk that when the phone rang, as it did at that moment, he had to cast aside a sheaf of papers in order to pick up the receiver.

"Yes, dear, I spoke to him," Morgan said into the receiver. "He's going to advertise it. Thirty damn years at this school, and this pipsqueak does that!"

Morgan became conscious that I was still in the corridor and used his walking stick to push the door shut. I moved on guiltily, feeling ashamed of my desire to know more. What was going on? Morgan fascinated me. He was part of an inner cabal of older teachers who seemed to form part of some kind of club: there was him, the Head of Geography, Mr Symes, the Deputy Head, Mrs Jones, the Head of History, Mr Wilde, and the Head of Music, Mr Folland. This lot were forever in one another's offices, or laughing merrily in the staffroom on Friday lunch-time over glasses of wine – a ritual that seemed to have been going on since the dawning of the Stone Age – or discussing the next trip they would take. All of them went together with the children on the annual Easter ski trip, and to the Music Festival in France during the summer. Mr Morgan also arranged a couple of "archaeological trips" for his "Special Needs Students" – usually the brightest children in the sixth form – during the year.

I rarely spoke to any of these teachers – they were in their own enclosed world – but I knew that the management in the school, the Head, the other Deputy and the Senior Teacher, were not happy with Morgan's merry little travel club. I wasn't quite sure why they weren't happy, but I could guess it was something to do with diverting too many resources into school trips.

I was soon to discover the source of Morgan's discontent because, while I was checking my pigeon hole, I came across the Headteacher pinning up a notice on the staff bulletin board. I caught his eye, and he grinned at me. Mr Woodham was not like any Head I had come across: he was youngish – early forties was my guess – had a little quiff drooping over his forehead, and seemed quite a reasonable person. The kind of guy you might go down to the pub with and chat about the latest film releases. He pointed at his notice and said, "You should take a look at this."

He didn't linger for me to ask him any more, whisking out of the room with a kind of skipping dance. He seemed, quite unlike Morgan, exceptionally merry.

I looked at the notice board and realised what was going on:

"Teacher In Charge Of Study Skills. The above post is being advertised after the delegation of the task for organising School Trips to administrative staff. The post will bring with it 1 Responsibility point. Please ask the Headteacher's Personal Assistant for an application pack."

I drew breath. Wow! This was big news. This was massive news. Woodham had sacked Morgan from running school trips! No wonder the old boy was looking a bit peaky! The wind of change was truly sweeping through the school now.

Yolanda entered the staffroom in a bright black and white, stylishly cut top – she was just about the trendiest teacher I had come across. She swept her hair back behind her face and her eyes widened as I showed her the notice.

"Fuck," she said. "What's going to happen to old Morgan? Do you think he'll apply?"

"I don't know," I shrugged, adding with a nervous glance. "Woodham told me that I should look at the notice."

"He said you should look at the notice?" Yolanda exclaimed, gripping my arm. And then letting go, asked, "How did he say that? Did he say it with a wink, or was it like, you know, deadpan, non-committal?"

"I think he said it with a bit of wink," I said. "But of course, he might have said it like that to you too."

"Fuck he would," Yolanda exclaimed again. "He wants you boy. You've taught in Tower Hamlets. He wants someone like you to try and teach these kids some basic Study Skills. I couldn't do that. I'm too inexperienced."

"You're not. You're good. You're one of the best," I said.

"You're better. I mean, I haven't read as many books as you," she said.

I went over to the kitchen counter and tried to encourage, albeit in my subtlest fashion, Yolanda to say more nice things about me. My usual technique was to slag myself off – to say I wasn't a good teacher etc – and get her to reassure me that I was. She would reciprocate with exactly the same technique, and I would praise her. I always finished conversations with her on a high because we would attempt to outdo each other with praise.

They were peculiarly personal conversations which we didn't allow anyone else to listen to; our slightly absurd eulogies about each other would terminate the moment someone entered earshot. (Although they felt perfectly innocent, they weren't conversations I told my wife about at that time!)

We quickly shut up when Morgan entered the staffroom with his crony, Folland, the decrepit Music Master, a very rotund, sweaty man who, somewhat inexplicably, put bicycle clips around the upper sleeves of his shirt. Morgan stormed over to the noticeboard and thrust his walking stick at the job advertisement.

"That's it! School trips have gone to administrative staff.

And I've got to teach blasted Study Skills."

"I suppose that is what you have always taught. Study Skills," Folland said a little dubiously.

Morgan considered this comment for a moment. Wrinkling his forehead, he looked into Folland's eyes and something approaching illumination began to surface in his face – like a little crack of sunlight appearing over troubled waters.

"Yes. That's it. That's what my trips have done. Taught study skills. He'll have to give me the job. He will. He'd better," Morgan said, and then, seeing that Yolanda and I were lurking by the kitchen counter hovering over chipped cups of coffee, he approached us. I could tell his natural bonhomie was returning.

"I just don't see how anyone would have the nerve to apply for MY job," he pronounced, gazing at both of us intently.

Neither Yolanda, or I replied. Instead, we made our excuses and were gone. Outside, with the morning sun beaming down on us as we negotiated our way in between the incoming kids, we looked at each other with wide eyes.

"You're not going to apply, are you?" Yolanda asked again. This time her tone was uncertain. She didn't like Morgan, but I could tell she was a bit frightened of him. He was a thunderer, and he had a lot of old friends at the school. He wasn't someone to fall out with.

I shrugged. "Probably not, it looks like a crummy job anyway."

EMOTOPIA

Miraculously, amazingly, wonderfully, my form were still well behaved. They would fall silent when I looked at them. I would rarely, if ever, have to ask them to be quiet when I was calling out the register. Their docility meant that I could really try and educate them. I would take a newspaper into every registration and read out some story of interest to them.

Sometimes, I would even try out whacky and adventurous ideas. Today I was trialling a particularly crazy notion. I called out the register and smiled as they looked up at me with expectant faces.

"Year 7, I'm going to try an experiment this week. I'd like to set up a system which rewards people who make other people feel positive. We're only to run this programme for a week. It's just a pilot but, if it works, then maybe we'll try it for longer."

I asked the class to make some paper money called E-Notes, and each pupil signed their name on the E-Notes.

"Now, I bet you're wondering what these E-Notes are, aren't you? Well, they are what I would like to term 'Emotional Notes'. Every time someone does you a favour, helps you out, perhaps even smiles at you, I'd like you to give them an 'E-Note' as payment. The pupils with the most E-Notes at the end of the week will get a prize. Now, obviously, if I see that you've received all your E-Notes from your best friend, then I'll have to take that into consideration. What I am trying to do is to make you see that being nice people has real value."

I should really have tried this idea out in Tower Hamlets, where the kids really did need to learn how to treat each other nicely, but I was aware that there were internecine rivalries and squabbling within this class that bubbled out when I was not around.

"Perhaps, E-Notes could eventually replace the capitalist system. Perhaps we could found an economy that put a commercial value upon emotions rather than material products?" Melissa Cruickshank commented. She was far too brainy for her age group; her father was a solicitor who often wrote letters of complaint about Melissa not being stretched properly at school. I shuddered to think what the conversations they must have over dinner were like.

"Seems a stupid idea to me," Billy Johns said with a snarl. "Why can't we just get money?"

"Well, I will give prizes to those people who get more than twenty E-Notes," I said. "And I'd like to put Melissa and Billy in charge of keeping a total of the E-Notes each pupil gets, and to make sure there is no cheating."

Suddenly the class, who had been reasonably attentive before, looked at each other gleefully. Oh, the enthusiasm, the naivety of young kids! They were the best. It felt like I could get them to do anything!

The kids left the room gabbling away about the E-Notes idea. I even saw one kid give his first E-Note away; his mate agreed to carry his heavy sports bag. That wasn't quite what I had intended the E-Notes system to be for, but I had been vague about the whole thing, and hadn't laid down many ground rules. Still, those would come as the children played the game.

ON TRIAL FOR MURDER

The class had re-arranged the furniture before I even got there. This was a big day for them. The day when Charlotte Dymond's lover went on trial.

We had been reading the poem *The Ballad of Charlotte Dymond* by Charles Causley, which is about one of Cornwall's most celebrated ghosts, Charlotte Dymond. She was found murdered on the slopes of Roughtor, near Camelford on Sunday 14th April 1844. Her lover, a disabled farm labourer called Matthew Weekes was later hanged at Bodmin Gaol for the crime, though it is doubtful that he committed it. Her ghost is supposed to haunt the place where she was murdered.

Since Weekes' conviction was so dubious, we instigated a trial. I allowed the pupils to make up their own details because the information in the poem and the history books was rather sketchy. Henry was the leading barrister for the prosecution. I almost laughed out loud. He'd found some silly lawyer's wig from somewhere, and a gown. What a transformation! From being a stroppy, disaffected kid, he'd blossomed into one of the leading characters of the class. The counsel for the defence was Sheila, quite a timid girl. Her hands were shaking as she held her notes.

Everyone else had come in costume too. Some kids were still changing into their clothes. It was hilarious. I smothered my smiles because it all seemed so deadly serious to them. The chairs had been re-arranged into a courtroom; a section for the jury, a section for witnesses – who were most of the class – and a table for the judge, who was me. I waited for everyone to get ready.

In my sternest voice I said, "I demand silence in court!" Henry had helpfully brought along a hammer and I used that to knock on the table.

"We are all here today to discover whether Matthew Weekes is guilty of murder or not. Remember, members of the jury, you must believe beyond a reasonable doubt that he is guilty. I call forward the counsel for the prosecution to put their case, and the defence to follow."

Henry stepped forward, adjusted his wig and addressed the jury. Reading from his notes, he said, "On the evening of 14th April 1844, Matthew Weekes walked out with Charlotte Dymond and viciously murdered her. His footprints were found near the scene of the crime and her blood on his clothes. During this prosecution we will conclusively prove that he is a cold-blooded murderer."

Henry finished with a flourish and doffed his wig at the crowd.

Sheila then shuffled to her feet. She was very nervous, and had none of Henry's bravado, but as she started reading she grew in confidence.

"The defence for Matthew Weekes will conclusively prove that he was framed, that he came upon his murdered lover, and knelt down to comfort her as she lay dying. The defence will show that Matthew had no motive for killing her. Suspicious footprints were found near the crime that indicate another person could have murdered her."

She sat down, sweating, but proud she had spoken loudly and clearly, and come up with a good case. Witnesses were called: Charlotte Dymond's parents, Matthew's teachers, his adopted parents, his psychiatrist, shopkeepers from the town, the vicar, farm labourers.

We had debated about calling Charlotte's ghost but decided against this since she would most probably know who murdered her! As we had read the poem on which the trial was based, the class had investigated the structure of the rural, 19th-century society that Charlotte Dymond had inhabited.

It went really well, generally; there were some hesitations, and some of the witnesses were a little flat, but Henry could be relied upon to spice things up.

"I put it to you that YOU ARE LYING!" he said, as Matthew himself finally took the stand. "We have already heard from the shopkeepers that you are a known THIEF. And the Vicar says you never come to church."

Matthew was actually played by a girl, Samantha, because she had insisted she wanted to play a "psycho". She wobbled her eyes at Henry, and said, "I am not lying! Charlotte was a prozzy! She deserved all she got!"

Henry pounced upon this. "What do you mean she deserved all she got?"

"She was two-timing me. She was going out with lots of other MEN," Samantha said, bursting out in a fit of giggles.

Titters rippled through the jury but everyone fell silent as Henry addressed her again.

"So you are admitting that you were angry with her? Did you want to kill her?"

Samantha shook her head. "I just wanted to tell her she was dirty."

"I put it to you that you said that and then YOU KILLED HER!"

Samantha stood up raging. "You can't say that! I'll get you too!"

"Me too?"

"You think you're so cool, standing there, but I'll get you."

This appeared to unnerve Henry because there seemed to be some hidden meaning behind it. He faltered and then sat down. The defence stepped up.

At the end of the trial, the class were asked to say whether they thought Matthew was guilty or not, and, to my astonishment, given the strength of the prosecutor's case, said that he was innocent.

When the bell rang, I asked Henry to stay behind. He seemed glum as he packed his wig, notes and books into his bag. I praised him. I had been careful not to congratulate him too much in front of the class.

"I think the class were mad not to find Matthew guilty," I said.

"Oh, they just wanted to get at me. Those girls, Samantha and her mates, they go out with the hard lads, and they got put up to it," he said, with a remarkable degree of equanimity.

"They shouldn't be doing that. But you're doing the right thing not to get upset by it. Here, I'll sign your merit book for that performance. You deserve five merits I think," I said.

He brightened at this, and produced his homework diary where I signed his merits. This was a reward system that most schools have whereby kids get merit points for doing good work; they receive prizes at the end of the year for getting over 50 merits.

I thought about the class ganging up on Henry as I walked into the staffroom for coffee break. I didn't want the same thing happening to me among my peer group and this was a definite possibility if I went for "Mr Morgan's job". Mrs Lee was knitting and chatting away about it with Mrs Malmesbury over their cups of tea.

"I always said to him that he had to do more than take the children on school trips. Always the same children, and always the same trip. Digging for old bits of broken crockery. Metal-detecting."

"But that was his post, Teacher in Charge of School Trips," Grace said. "He was only doing his job."

"It's gone to administration staff now," Mrs Lee said.

Yolanda found me by the pigeon holes and demanded to hear more news. I didn't have any to tell.

"So you haven't made a decision yet? Remember Morgan's look, heh?"

I considered my position yet again as I returned to my classroom.

"Yo, dudes, this is the biz. This is the rocking Kubla Khan FM here, and I is yer rocking MC, giving you the low-down on the top holiday place in the world! Get yer ass down to the pass in Xanadu! Don't muss up yer life, and come and see the man, himself, Kubla Khan. A better leader, there ain't. He's got women wailing for their demon lovers, sunny caves of ice, and the fittest chicks this side of China."

Karl Jefferson's presentation was replete with sound-effects, suitable ducking and diving hand, head movements, and machismo strutting up and down. I had to admit to myself that his rap interpretation of the task I had set wasn't what I had quite expected. Having read Coleridge's poem *Kubla Khan* to these twelve-year-olds, I had asked them to devise a radio travel programme which discussed the most interesting features of the fantastical land that Coleridge evokes. It was an ambitious task; the poem isn't an easy one. But Karl's eyes lit up when I mentioned doing something connected with the radio. He was even willing to work in a group that included a couple of girls, and what he termed a 'geek'.

The class applauded and Karl beamed back a rap-star smile. However, a couple of days later, Karl's success seemed to have made him far too cocky. I was walking across the playground with Yolanda when he shouted at me, from a jeering knot of tough kids who were hanging about on the edge of the playing fields: "Yo, Gilbert, lover man, how's it going?"

This sort of familiarity made me tense up in those days. I now handle this kind of thing by asking for due deference in a smiley, jokey way. But then I stalked over to Karl, and shouted at him, "Excuse me, you don't talk to me like that! I am Mr Gilbert to you, not, not…"

Karl's lips were tensed together. He didn't like being told off in front of his older, more hardened mates – some of whom I knew had had skirmishes with the police. But as he saw that I was floundering because I didn't want to pronounce the name he had given me, a grin spread across his face, and he said, "Not a lover man! Not lover man!"

"Karl, you're coming with me right now! I won't have this insolence!" I said, trying to find a way out of this conundrum. I could feel Yolanda behind me, probably thinking I was a complete prat for letting this Year 8 pupil "diss" me so badly.

Karl shook his head, winking at me with disdain. "I ain't going with you, you ain't gonna get me to do nothing."

This was terrible. A minor little piece of name-calling in the playground was turning into a major incident. And all in front of Yolanda! Fortunately, it was she who saved me from myself by gently touching my arm, and suggesting that we retreat until a more opportune time arose to deal with this.

"Karl, Mr Gilbert will see you later about all of this," she said. I followed her away from the hooting group of Karl's friends, my face stinging from the boy's insubordination. Once we were out of their earshot, Yolanda told me that I shouldn't have confronted him in front of his friends; I had left him with no choice but to put me down.

"But I've tried so hard with that kid, I've really encouraged him Yolanda," I said. "He shouldn't have spoken to me like that."

"Francis, come on, get real. The kid was with a group who don't give a flying fuck if the cops nick them. What's he going to do when you ask for a bit more respect, bow down and pray to you?" she said.

I mulled over her words that morning, and then, to my surprise, Karl came to find me that lunch-time. I was in the computer room running a magazine club – for which I got given £2.50 and a free lunch.

The group consisted mainly of girls from my tutor group, plus Hal, from my Year 7 group who came along as well. They were all working on a summer edition of the magazine, to be published in July. Karl didn't exude the sneering bravado that he had shown at lunch; his shoulders were droopy, and he wouldn't look me in the eye.

"Miss Williams said I should come and see you," he said. I glanced at the group. They were all busily typing away at the computers. This would be a good time to talk to him. We were on the top floor of the school. Outside, a pure blue sky lifted my spirits. Down below, children were laughing and playing around. I could easily sort this out if I didn't lose my temper.

"Is there something you want to say to me?" I asked Karl. He bunched his hands into fists. He seemed quite angry with me.

"Sir, I mean, I ain't dissing you or nothing, but you got it all wrong. I mean, you got it wrong," he said.

He waited for my response. He was half-expecting me to get cross with him, I thought. But I remained calm. Now that we were out of the context of the playground, and Yolanda was nowhere in sight, I could relax.

"What do you mean?"

Karl looked at me now. His shoulders straightened, and he leaned closer to me. A familiar cheeky grin spread across his face. He whispered: "I mean, ya dunno what lover man means do you?"

This puzzled me. "Well, I have a pretty good idea," I whispered back.

"No, but ya dunno what it really means, do ya?"

"Of course, I do, it's someone, well a man I suppose, who has lots of lovers. Not a great thing to say to a married man like me," I whispered in all seriousness.

Karl let out a tiny laugh. His eyes were full of mirth and embarrassment.

"Yeah, there's that, but it's more than that, it means something good," he said, "Do you know what I mean?"

I didn't quite. But I nodded my head anyway. It wasn't really a topic that I wanted to pursue at greater length; the question I was really interested in was whether or not Karl was completing his homework.

"Hey, you know, I thought that Xanadu FM thing was great," I said. "It looks like you worked hard on that." Karl nodded.

"But sometimes, I don't get much other stuff out of you, particularly your homework!" I said in a light-hearted tone.

Karl shrugged. "I'm busy man!"

"Busy doing what? What happens when you go home?" Karl didn't reply at first.

"I gotta help my mum. I gotta look after my sisters."

"How old are they?"

Karl replied that they were three and six. I knew from Yolanda that the children in his family all had different fathers; but now, by questioning Karl in the seclusion of this sunlit computer room, with its aquamarine, high windows, I could gather a better idea of what was going on. According to his own account, which probably wasn't that reliable, Karl was being the Dad at home.

He lived in a council flat near the school, and didn't have the room, the time, or the environment there to do any homework. His sisters were always yelling and rushing about, he said. And his mum just wanted to stay in the kitchen, making soup and listening to the radio. I got the picture of a mother who was loving and kind, but struggling to cope. It sounded like she was good at feeding and clothing the children, but didn't quite know what to do with them after that. There seemed to be no sign of a father, or fathers, or boyfriends. I got the impression that it wasn't a chronically deprived home, but nor was it ideal.

Karl was clean, well dressed, and healthy, and he was aware of the dangers that awaited him. This became clear over the course of the next year, because he started coming to the magazine club to do some of his homework, and he would tell me what some of his so-called friends were up to.

"They want me to smoke, you know?" he said once. "I say Nah, I don't wanna, but then they diss me, and so I have a drag, but I don't like it."

The following year, he stopped coming to the club, and I saw that he was properly immersed in the gang culture of the school. He got excluded a couple of times for smoking. I thought about trying to speak to him, but by then, I was so busy with other more bureaucratic matters, which at the time I thought were more important, that I didn't actually make the effort.

But that was all in the future. At this moment in time, four months into my teaching career at Humbards, my biggest worries were rather Will Jenkins and Albert Tench. It was a few days before the Key Stage 3 English test. The class would have two papers to sit; a reading and writing paper, and a Shakespeare paper. The whole thing was making me quite nervous: these would be my first results in the school. I thought – erroneously, as it turned out – that I would be judged on the results of these children. It made me even more a control freak than I was with my other classes.

The class had listened to the audio tape of *Romeo and Juliet*, and completed detailed questions on the two scenes that they would be specifically tested upon. We were now going to do some revision using the Mindmapping™ technique.

I drew a Mindmap™ on the board based on the character of Capulet, Juliet's tyrannical father. Mindmaps™ are an advanced version of spider diagrams which can help pupils understand the basic principles of a subject, as well as assist with taking notes. You always put the central idea for the Mindmap™ in the middle of the page. (In this case, it was Capulet.) Then you put big branches, showing the main points to consider, coming out of the centre.

So I was trying to teach the class five key ideas about Capulet: that he was a control freak, bad-tempered, wealthy, prejudiced but also sympathetic towards Romeo. These central ideas then had off-shoots where details were added in to provide more evidence for those points – that Capulet was a control freak, for example, was endorsed by the fact that Juliet was always expected to obey him. I used the arrow symbol to indicate important information about the character, and other symbols to emphasize key points.

I have found Mindmapping™ a very useful teaching tool over the years: it puts the emphasis upon the student to arrive at understandable notes for themselves. I always preface my notes with the comment that pupils MUST UNDERSTAND their own notes, it is no good copying mine verbatim. The whole point about Mindmapping™ is that pupils must develop their own personalised notes which they themselves may understand but other people may not. I encouraged the pupils to use colours and pictures to help remember key concepts.[6]

Instead of producing a Mindmap™ to elucidate Capulet's role, however, Will Jenkins did a clever pastiche of my own Mindmap™, showing that he understood the key concepts and that he was intent upon tormenting me. It revealed what he thought I was guilty of: control-freakery, strutting about

---

[6] Mindmapping ™. It is massive subject with a whole methodology and I have only touched upon it here. Read any book by Tony Buzan for more information.

my classroom, being moody, prejudiced, having no money and a crap car.

I wasn't very happy when I looked at Jenkins's Mindmap™. I picked it up and scrutinised it. He was grinning maliciously at me, and widening his eyes in a mock-mad stare, like the one Jack Nicholson has in *The Shining*. I swiftly ripped the page out of his book, and told him to write a proper Mindmap™, otherwise I would report him to the Head of Year. He protested, and his friend Tench, joined in.

"You can't tear my book. That's vandalism!" he said. Tench quickly echoed his words.

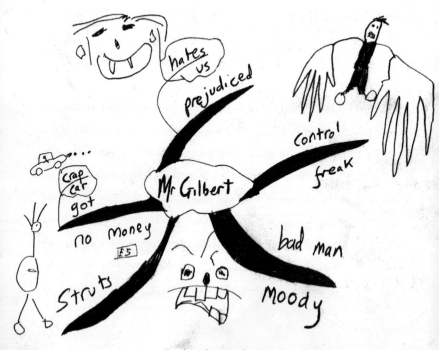

Jenkins's mindmap

"You've got a test in two days time, get on with the work," I replied.

I left the pair of them muttering about my "vandalism" as I wandered to the front of the class. I thought that, as bad behaviour went, it wasn't that serious. In my other school, I had been told to fuck off, I'd had kids smoking in my class-room, and been hit. This was nothing. So why did it get to me? Jenkins was bright and articulate, and he knew my psycholog-ical weak spots, and appeared to enjoy probing them like a sadistic doctor poking into an open wound to see where the pain was. Did I really come across like Capulet to the children? Was I that bad? Was that why I kept order – because I was a bastard?

INTUITION AT LUNCH

I always managed to hook up with Yolanda during lunch-times, and now, today, we had a real reason to meet. She rushed up to me as I was putting my borstal tray down on the table. Our table was clearly demarcated as a "teachers' table" – no pupils sat at it – but it was situated just behind the sixth form's tables. I noticed Jemima Killen chatting away to her friends there. I wondered for a moment whether it was wise to talk here, but thought that actually nothing we were going to say was of much interest to sixth formers – who seemed to have only clubs, pubs, skimpy tops and drugs on their minds. Mr Morgan's job was of virtually no interest to them.

Yolanda produced a "dieting food supplement" sachet from her bag, and poured it into a glass of water. She stirred it vigorously as she whispered with wide eyes, "Morgan's on the warpath. He went to the Head. Apparently, the secretaries could hear shouting. He's lost it! The man has lost it! He took his walking stick with him, and waved it around."

"Oh my God," I said.

Yolanda sipped her diet drinkk, and I ate my Cornish pasty and lukewarm baked beans. Things felt very grave somehow. Heavy. Nasty.

"I'm not sure that I should go for it," I said.

To my surprise, Yolanda agreed whole-heartedly with this tentative comment, which had actually been a cue for her to contradict me.

She put her hand on mine and then took it off quickly. "Don't do it, Francis. It's going to spell trouble. I just have a feeling about it."

"A feeling?"

"Intuition, if you like. My mum had the power of clairvoyance, you know. She was from St Lucia. People used to go to her for advice. Still do, except that she's in Balham now. I think I inherited a bit of it from her," she said. "Don't do it."

This injunction pissed me off. Yolanda had been so

encouraging before, and now she was using her hocus-pocus to try to stop me going ahead with it. Why should I let Morgan intimidate me? I wasn't scared of Morgan or any of his cronies.

"Thanks," I said weakly. I tipped my pasty and beans into the rubbish bin, and returned to my classroom.

ADVICE FROM THE PUPILS

"What's the matter, sir? You look a bit depressed today," Jemima said, stretching her arms up to the ceiling. She was always thrusting her breasts in my direction whenever she addressed me. Stretching her arms above her head was her favourite; it meant that the whole of her upper frame was lifted up and pushed forward. This, coupled with her inevitably tight-fitting tops, made the whole process of talking to her quite unnerving. I still hadn't told her to wear less revealing outfits, but nor had anyone else in the school, apparently. The only person who complained about her clothes was Yolanda, who had been typically forthright in her assessment: "Jemima, why are your boobs always falling out of your clothes?"

Yolanda didn't teach Jemima and received short shrift. "What's it got to do with you?"

But now, I sensed that Jemima was being sympathetic towards me.

"Do I look depressed?" I asked.

Most of the class were working on their coursework essays on Thomas Hardy's poetry. They'd have to hand them in in a couple of weeks' time; they were very important, forming nearly a quarter of their final mark for A-Level English Literature. Only Josh and Rob, the two boys in the class, and Jemima had other things on their minds; the other girls were dutifully scribbling, reading, scribbling and reading. But it was quite boring for me who was used to frenetic activity in the classroom. So I strolled over to Jemima and the boys.

"I hear you're going for Morgan's job," Jemima whispered.

"What? How do you know that?" This genuinely surprised me. How did Jemima know anything about Morgan's job?

"Morgan told me," Jemima said with glowing eyes. Then she winked. Josh and Rob grinned. What did this lot know?

"He told you?" I wrinkled my forehead, quite puzzled.

"Don't forget he teaches us. I mean he doesn't actually teach us, but he does talk to us about archaeology and whatever is on his mind," Jemima said. Josh and Rob nodded.

"I thought you were supposed to be reading *Jane Eyre* with him," I said.

"We read that ages ago. We just have a chat now. He's not like you. I mean, we don't have to do work."

"I know a lot about the rituals and the habits of the Ancient Greeks. Plato and that crap," Josh said dryly.

"And excavating on Mount Olympus," Rob added.

Morgan sounded a lot like the teachers I had had at the minor public school I had been to: eccentric but bizarrely inspiring. Nevertheless, it was a bit worrying that he was mouthing off about me to the pupils. Or was he? I only had their word for it, and I knew information from kids wasn't to be trusted. Besides, how could Morgan possibly know I was going for the job? I hadn't even decided myself.

"I think you should go for it," Jemima said.

"Yeah, go for it," Rob urged me.

THE TRAP

These sixth formers' exhortations came back to me as I was walking home; I felt fatally encouraged by them. I felt as if they were more on my side than any teachers were. They knew I could do a good job. And they were the ones that really knew the truth about teachers. Or did they? Was it just a trap?

A WEEK LATER

"So, Francis, what makes you think that you are qualified for this job?" Tony Woodham asked me.

My cheeks were growing hot. It suddenly seemed very warm in the Headteacher's office. Four pairs of eyes stared at me. I scanned four serious, tense faces. No one was smiling.

No one looked like they were having fun. Everyone was scribbling notes onto pro-formas attached to clipboards.

"Er..." I hesitated. Why had I applied for this job? There was only one real reason. I wanted to be important. I wanted to have status. I didn't want to be a lowly mainscale teacher anymore; I wanted to strut around like Mr Morgan did, looking purposeful while flourishing my walking stick. Well, I wouldn't have a walking stick; maybe I'd have a clipboard, or something else distinctive and slightly intimidating.[7]

"I feel really committed to improving pupils' study skills. I think it is the most important area to be addressed in the curriculum; pupils' ability to take notes, to organise their thoughts, and to set targets, are crucial if we are going to improve results in the school," I said swiftly.

I could have carried on. From feeling completely dried up, the verbiage was now streaming out: I felt lots of teacher jargon bursting into my head like a fountain. However, while his entourage continued frantically scribbling on to their

---

[7] Props for important teachers: every really important teacher has some distinctive prop which indicates that they are both individual and imposing. Confident P.E. teachers carry whistles around their necks, blowing upon them whenever they see anything untoward. Some Headteachers and Deputy Heads carry around a clipboard permanently, jotting down insidious notes as they traverse the school. Female teachers have the great advantage of having the right to carry around vast handbags bulging with lots of books and papers. Male teachers sometimes opt for briefcases. In my case, I have found my very own prop which I am known for: my hefty mobile phone-cum-electronic-personal organiser. I place it in a wallet and attach it to my belt every morning. It makes me feel like a gunslinger because of the way it swings about my hips.

pro-formas, I paused. I tried to gauge from the rapidity and nature of their scribbling whether they were on my side or not. The Headteacher, Woodham, seemed a little non-committal with his notes – he was always quite a distant character, though, and this behaviour was not indicative of anything. Jane Henry, the parent governor, looked a bit confused and was probably trying to sort out her thoughts, while Ismael Waldenstein, the Head of the Upper School, appeared enthusiastic about me by the way he was writing flowing, copious notes. Mrs Jones, the Deputy Head, in contrast, was digging her pen deeply into the paper; she really didn't want me to get the job. She was a major pal of Morgan's.

It was Mrs Jones who turned to me next, and asked, "So how would you hope to deliver your study skills curriculum?"

This was the hardest question to answer because from what I had read of the job there appeared to be no set lesson time for study skills. Nor was there much money. Nor any text books. I guessed that it was probably a question of cajoling teachers to do a bit of it in their lessons.

"I would carry out an audit of the school's schemes of work, then, working with Heads of Department, I would see where study skills could be implemented. Then we'd need to train staff, and following that ask them to deliver it in lessons," I said.

Mrs Jones blinked and then peered severely over her glasses: "And how do you propose to do that when there is no money for study skills in the budget?"

Mr Woodham coughed. "I think, Mrs Jones, there will be some money available," he added. "Well, thank you, Francis. You've clearly thought about this. Do you have any questions for us?"

My heart started beating even faster because I did want to make a point. Perhaps it was the real reason why I had applied for the job – out of sheer bloody-mindedness. "I've come under a lot of pressure not to apply for this job. Are you looking for a more experienced member of staff?"

"It is a job for an experienced member of staff," Mrs Jones began, but was interrupted by Mr Woodham. "However, we do regard you as experienced. You've taught in Tower Hamlets, and seen a bit. I'm sorry that you've felt under pressure not to apply, but I am grateful that you have. Thanks for trying."

Mr Woodham stood up at this point, indicating that the interview was at a close.

"Thanks for considering me," I said, getting up. No one else looked up at me; they were too busy scribbling. Everything felt very, very serious. It seemed even more so when I walked out of the Head's office and saw Mr Morgan waiting in a cushioned chair. His face was white and impassive. He didn't acknowledge me, nor I him.

We'd already spoken a few days before, when he'd approached me by the staff pigeon holes. "So I hear you are applying for my job. I'm not sure what I think of that," he'd said, and walked away. Perhaps, it wasn't this comment that had hurt most, just his determination not to acknowledge me at all when we passed each other in the corridor.[8]

I think if I experienced a similar interview now, I would feel quite depressed. But I was young, and not the veteran of interviews I have become. The tenseness of the atmosphere added to the excitement and suspense.

Yolanda snuck out of her classroom when I passed by, leaving her Year 9 to chat while she got the "goss". I told her every detail.

"Sounds freaky! Something freaky is going to happen, I can just feel it. I think you might get it!" she giggled.

A little tremor passed through me. I hadn't actually considered this possibility until now. Yes, perhaps I would shaft old Morgan and get the damn job. Then I would be important. Very important. And I was half his age.[9]

---

[8] <u>Knowing who to say hello to.</u> This is a major stress in every teacher's life because teachers know so many people. Do you say hello to every pupil you teach? To every teacher you know? In which case, you'd be saying nothing but hello every time you crossed the playground. So most teachers in secondary schools usually opt for saying hello to a select few: departmental colleagues, favourite pupils, the Headteacher if they're sensible. Morgan was one of the select few I had always said hello to. His refusal to acknowledge me was a real snub.

[9] <u>Uppity youngsters.</u> Now that I am older, and have observed ambitious young teachers, teachers considerably younger than myself, climbing the greasy pole, I can appreciate just how repellent I must have been. However, youth often brings hope into institutions as well as arrogance and bravado. Without ambitious youngsters, schools would feel very defeated places.

A REVENGER'S TRAGEDY?

Although the school had arranged for my classes to be covered, I decided to teach out the remainder of the day while I waited for the result. It was pretty amazing: the fact is that I enjoyed teaching! I strolled into my Year 8 class and told the supply teacher he could go: he was particularly pleased with me because he would be paid for doing nothing.

The class were completing a spelling and grammar worksheet that was specially designed for cover classes. Dull, dull, dull. I had a whole new unit of work I wanted to start with them. I wrote a word in big letters on the board: REVENGE.

"What does that word make you think of?"

Jefferson stuck his hand up straight away. "Getting even. Stuffing the other guy. Whacking him. Taking him out," he said gleefully, doing fake punches into the air.

"Good, good," I said confidently. There would have been a time when his aggressive comments would have made me more defensive, but not now. I felt in command of the situation. "Write it all down in your Mindmap™!"

I asked them to think of any stories or films that they knew that were about revenge. Jefferson said he'd seen Clint Eastwood's *Unforgiven*, even though it was an "18", and he was twelve.

"It's wicked, guy, these bastards kill his friend, and then

he gets them. Pow, pow, pow!"

"OK," I said. "Now I want you to imagine what you would do if the ghost of a good friend visits you late at night and asks you to get revenge on someone you know because he says he's been murdered. The thing is, you don't really believe in ghosts, and also you might not believe in revenge. You are a Christian. Jesus said that you should never take revenge. You should always forgive people's sins. So what do you do? What I want you to do is try and write out an outline of a story that includes this situation."

This was what made teaching fun. I was genuinely interested in seeing what stories the kids would come up with, and what their take on *Hamlet* – the play I was covertly introducing to them – would be.

A few of the students came up with some original ideas. One storyline was particularly striking; it involved a football player who was killed by a rival. The football player then came back as a ghost and asked the goalkeeper to get revenge on the player.

For some reason, the scenario stuck in my head, and began to haunt me. There was no news about the appointment at the end of the day so I walked home with the *revenger's tragedy* on my mind. If I did get the job, would Morgan take his revenge upon me?

***

The next morning I learnt that the interview panel were re-convening during the first two lessons in order to find the right person. This was unprecedented. I'd never come across such long deliberations for such a comparatively lowly post before. What was going on?

Was it just co-incidence that I had chosen to teach revenge at this point? When the lesson was over, the Headteacher's face appeared outside my classroom, and he told me that he wanted me to come back to the office. I followed him without a word. The door closed behind me, and Mrs Jones spoke with a fixed smile on her face. "Mr Gilbert, we'd like to appoint you Study Skills Co-ordinator. Would you like to accept?"

I tried my best to sound enthusiastic when I said, "Yes, most definitely, yes." But my words were edged with doubt. What had I let myself in for? Was I now the villain in Mr Morgan's Revenger's Tragedy? Was he old Hamlet, and was I Claudius? Where was Hamlet himself?

STAFFROOM TELEPATHY

I returned to the staffroom at the end of break, wondering if I would find anyone there; I knew most of the staff would be teaching. There was no one around except Mrs Lee and Grace

Malmesbury, who were packing up their knitting. Mrs Lee picked up a shopping bag full of books, her knitting bag and her handbag and lurched towards the door with her load. She winked at me.

"Well done sonny, you've clearly got a bit of spark. Certainly put the wind up old Morgan!" she said gleefully. Grace cackled behind her. "He was certainly thrashing his walking stick around when he came in here!"

I wrinkled my forehead. How did they know that I had got the job already? Did they have some sort of telepathic empathy with the walls of the institution that enabled them, like the witches in *Macbeth*, to know everything? Or did they have a spy on the interview panel?

I should have asked them but I didn't. I didn't want to appear ruffled. I wanted to be cool. Ice cool. Take everything in my stride. Show that I would be an efficient, effective manager.

However, my face began to twitch when I looked in my pigeon-hole. It had been filled with an enormous quantity of paper. I flicked through it and saw that virtually none of it was relevant to me; someone had gathered together all the useless bits of paper in the staffroom – the union magazines, the PTA news, the results of a Home Economics survey – and stuffed them into my pigeon hole. Had it been deliberate or was it just a misunderstanding? I couldn't exactly tell, but I felt it was an indication that I wasn't the most popular person on the staff at that moment.

THE VEXED TALE OF JEMIMA'S COURSEWORK ESSAY

Jemima put her hand up. Even though it was a hot day, she was not wearing her customary tight-fitting top. Her torso was demurely covered with a zipped-up tracksuit jacket. Her lips were pursed and her hair tied back in a severe pony-tail. She wasn't wearing any make-up, as she normally did.

"What's this sir?" she pointed at the essay that was in front of her entitled: "In what ways does Thomas Hardy explore the theme of love in his poetry?" I looked down at her neatly written, if uninspired essay. "How come you gave me a B grade?"

"Well, I marked you according to the syllabus, taking into account the criteria necessary for a B grade. You have to explore in an analytical fashion the themes of a literary work. That's what you've done. It's a good essay."

"How come I didn't get a B plus? You gave Martina a B plus, but you gave me a B."

"I thought that Martina's essay had the edge over yours. She'd explored the issues a bit more analytically," I said. Martina, who was sitting next to her, grinned. "I was more analytical than you Jem!" she simpered.

"You weren't. I included loads of analysis. I don't get it," Jemima said, snatching Martina's essay out of her hands.

"Hey! Stop that. That's my essay, not yours," Martina said, attempting to retrieve the essay from her friend. Jemima wrinkled her forehead and scanned the essay, chucking the pages back to Martina as she did so. Her cavalier tossing of the papers was not respectful.

"Jemima, don't do that. That's Martina's coursework essay. You can't just chuck it around the room," I said.

"But it's not fair, she gets a B plus, and I got a B. I know my essay is just as good as hers! It's a B plus."

"What difference does it make – a B, or a B plus? It hardly makes any difference in the grand scheme of things!" I said impatiently. "Look, I'll get a second opinion if you like."

"You mean you'll put it up?" Jemima asked hopefully, unzipping her jacket.

"I'll get a second opinion," I said.

After the lesson, I took the essay to Mrs Lee. I didn't say to her that it was the first time I had taught A-Level coursework, but just explained that I would value her expert opinion. She beamed and took the essay from me.

She got back to me the next day with a jaded look on her face. "Oh dear, I fear this is more like a D grade essay than a B, Francis. What have you been telling this class about

Thomas Hardy? There are several misconceptions about his poetry here. To say that he was almost happy about his wife's death is, quite frankly, outrageously wrong. And there are so many grammatical mistakes. She does split her infinitives, doesn't she? And subject/verb agreement is not easy for her. A definite D grade! You really will have to get her to re-write it. And I think I should perhaps look at all your coursework. We don't want the board marking us down. The humiliation of it!"

My heart sank. Mrs Lee was most put out. This was the last thing that I wanted. Had I really misinterpreted Hardy so badly? And what the hell was a split infinitive? And I felt a bit shaky about my subject-verb agreements as well! Was I totally incompetent? Did I really know how to mark? And what was I going to tell Jemima?

I took the essay from Mrs Lee with trepidation. I felt terrible. "I'm sorry," I muttered to her. "I'll get her to re-write it."

Mrs Lee was already engrossed in her knitting, and appeared to feel that the conversation was at an end. Her sudden switch to the knitting made me hope against my better instincts that she would perhaps forget about asking for the rest of the coursework. But deep down, I knew that she would definitely ask all the children to re-write their essays. Particularly since she disagreed with one of the points we had made in class – a point that the students had argued for, and I had agreed with, after thought – that Hardy was secretly pleased that his wife had died. In the class's view it had enabled him to objectify her, to quantify her influence, to re-connect with the memory of the youthful Emma.

But what was I going to do with Jemima? Perhaps foolishly, I didn't think too hard about this. I would get her to re-write it. She'd moan, but since Mrs Lee had said she was a D grade, she'd have to accept it.

The next lesson, I told Jemima the news. She froze.

"It's what?"

"Mrs Lee thinks it's a D grade and she wants to correct the grammar," I said somewhat coyly. I could see immediately that this wasn't going to be straightforward.

"What about Martina's essay?" Jemima said.

"I didn't show her Martina's essay. Martina didn't want a second opinion, you did."

"I didn't say I wanted a second opinion. I said I wanted a B plus. And you tell me that this is a D grade. I don't believe this. You picked on me because I argued with you, didn't you?"

This made me cross. I felt that Jemima was re-interpreting the past to her own advantage. My nostrils flared. "Look, Mrs Lee has kindly shown you where to correct the piece. You correct it and then we'll see."

"But you said it was B grade! Do you know how to mark or what?"

"Jemima! You don't speak to me like that! You re-write the essay or leave it at a D grade! And that's that. Now we have to get on with studying Seamus Heaney!" I thundered.

Jemima's lip quivered, and tears started rolling down her cheeks. She then put her head on the desk and appeared to sob quietly for the rest of the lesson. Martina looked distraught. She asked whether she should take Jemima to the medical room just as I was getting started with introducing the series of "Bog Poems" written by Seamus Heaney. Heaney writes in visceral detail about the discovery of a number of dead bodies in the bogs of Denmark. The poet believed that a few of the ancient bodies were the victims of ritual sacrifice.

"Heaney was fascinated by the idea of the scapegoat," I said somewhat queasily. "The person who was blamed for a society's ills."

The poems suddenly took on a different resonance now. Was I going to be thrown, slashed and scarred, into an educational bog? I shook my head. I was just being ridiculous.

Jemima's desk was wet with tears at the end of the lesson. I felt terrible but I thought that I had done the right thing. Rather than having the whole class in uproar about having to re-write their essays, it was better to have a bit of grief with Jemima.

A NASTY PHONECALL

The next day, Mrs Lee hollered for me in the corridor. It was early morning. A light, summery mist was rising off the grass in the quadrangle. It was going to be a beautiful day. "Mr Gilbert, Mr Gilbert! You're wanted on the telephone."

I followed Mrs Lee into the tiny room where her office was. Mrs Lee didn't know who it was, nor was she particularly interested. She appeared to be in the middle of some arduous GCSE paperwork. I picked up the receiver expecting to hear Yolanda in the Humanities Block wanting to gossip about staffroom intrigues. Instead I got a shock. "Hello, this is Mrs Killen. Jemima's mother. Is that Mr Gilbert?"

Her tone was brusque to say the least.

"Yes," I said. "Do you want anything?"

"I certainly do. I am not happy Mr Gilbert. I am very unhappy in fact. Jemima has been making some very serious allegations against you. Some VERY SERIOUS allegations and I need to talk to you immediately."

"Yes, certainly," I gulped.

"When? When can I put these allegations before you?"

"Well, I'm teaching all day. Perhaps after school?"

"Where shall I come?"

"To the school?" I said, my mind was in a daze, and I wasn't thinking all that clearly.

Mrs Killen sighed. "I know that, but where? To the office? Main reception? Shall I meet you there?"

The phone line went dead. I was left holding the receiver. Mrs Lee was blithely getting on with her paperwork. I looked at her and wondered whether I should say what was going on. She was my Head of Department after all. And, in a certain sense, she had got me into this mess. But I really, really didn't want to share this with her.

I felt that she wouldn't understand, and I'd end up listening to her rabbit on for hours about split infinitives and subject/verb agreement. (I was now very familiar with these terms and a thousand others because I had spent the whole weekend with an old-fashioned grammar book.)

I rushed from the office and tried to find Yolanda. I needed to speak with her desperately. She was the only one that I really trusted. What the fuck were these allegations that Jemima was making?

I found Yolanda with her tutor group making displays for the Lower School block. I indicated with urgent eyes that I needed to speak with her. She put down her sugar paper and gave it to one of the kids. She immediately sensed my panic and put her hand on my wrist outside the classroom.

"Calm down, Francis, what is it? What's going on? You look mad," she whispered.

I shut the door to the classroom so that the kids wouldn't

90

hear us. "It's this parent. Jemima's. Making allegations," I said, swallowing hard. I realised that if Jemima really was making serious allegations, then I could be suspended from my job, even though I was totally innocent and I had done nothing.

"What? Calm down! Try and make sense!"

I took a deep breath and recounted to Yolanda the whole rigmarole about the coursework, Mrs Lee's intervention, and what Mrs Killen had said. Yolanda's eyes widened.

"You'd better go and see the Head."

"Do you think?"

"Yeah, I would. I mean it's better for you to go first rather than Mrs Killen go to him. You'll always be on the defensive then."

"But what if Mrs Killen doesn't go to the Head, then he'll never know I was an idiot about marking the coursework," I said.

"Being an idiot about coursework is no crime! It doesn't matter. Woodham knows the score."

"But Mrs Lee more or less said my coursework was a disgrace," I said. "And I've just got this Study Skills job. I don't want to look incompetent."

"It's better being incompetent than having to fight false allegations on your own. You've got to tell him the truth. And Mrs Lee can go to hell! She's a silly old moo!"

I laughed. This was the first time Yolanda had really

expressed her true feelings about Mrs Lee. She didn't like her at all. I blinked my eyes. I was grateful for Yolanda's words of advice. She was right. I had to go to see Woodham. Either way, he had to deal with Mrs Killen. This was serious. I didn't want to see Mrs Killen alone, and I certainly didn't want Mrs Lee's "support". I had to be seen to have the top honcho's backing with this one.

"Go and tell him now. I'll cover your register," Yolanda said.

I walked straight to Woodham's office. His door was open. It normally was. I liked Woodham. He was easily the most approachable Head I had come across. I didn't sense he was in the game of wielding power just for the sake of it. He had a Cary Grant quiff, a love of all things American, and his favourite band was The Doors. He was cool.

He shut the door behind me and asked me to sit down. I explained the situation to him, leaving nothing out. I even told him that I was reluctant to show the rest of my coursework to Mrs Lee because I knew she would ask me to get it re-written and I felt that this would undermine my authority with the rest of the class.

He smiled and put his feet up on the desk. "I wouldn't worry about it, Francis. The girl may have a crush on you and have made up a lot of stuff. I'll talk to the mother and get back to you. Leave it with me."

92

He swung his feet off his desk and guided me to the door, patting me on the back. "It'll be fine. Don't worry about it."

CHARADE

But I did worry! I was consumed with anxiety all day. I was grateful that I was teaching, though. It took my mind off what Mrs Killen was going to tell Woodham.

My Year 9 class was a bit unnerving because, as a post-Key Stage 3 test exercise, I had asked the class to devise their own murder mysteries. They were working in groups of six and each group had to come up with a scenario, a selection of characters and someone who had been murdered. They had to bring in evidence and present the "murder" to the class, without revealing who the murderer was. The class then had to cross-examine them in order to find out who the real murderer was.

Everyone was keen for it. Again, I couldn't help marvelling at the way these kids organised themselves. I could give them an open-ended topic, without any proper worksheets, and slightly vague instructions, and they would invent the rules for themselves. I could never have done an exercise like this in my previous school in Tower Hamlets; there would have been chaos. It would have been an opportunity to fight.

For Jenkins it was another opportunity to play mind-games. His group's murder victim was a ginger-haired teacher called Gilbey who was hated by his pupils, the staff and the caretaker. This unscrupulous teacher loved giving detentions to innocent, harmless children, and stealing from the stock cupboard. It was all pretty slanderous, but, within the context of what was now happening, it felt harmless. While Jenkins was somehow straightforward, Jemima was not.

My next lesson was with the sixth formers. I didn't even acknowledge Jemima, who sat tight-lipped and sulky at the back of the class as we read and made notes on the bog people in Seamus Heaney's poems. The other girls in the group seemed similarly downcast. The only chipper people were Josh and Rob who volunteered to read and offered a lot of comments. They were really growing in confidence.

At the end of the lesson, they both approached me. It was lunch-time, and everyone else had disappeared. Rob appeared concerned. "Look sir, you should know that Mr Morgan is saying things about you." Mr Morgan was their other English teacher, who shared the A-Level set with me.

"He says that you don't know your grammar and that we should always get our essays checked with him," Josh said.

"I don't like him. He just talks about archaeology and ancient Greek philosophy. He doesn't really talk about the books we're reading," Rob added.

More bad news. I thanked Rob and Josh. They were my

mates. They knew the truth. But what about the other girls in the group? What was going on?

At the end of the day, I waited nervously in my classroom, trying to mark books. Woodham had told me he would catch Mrs Killen at the main reception and that I wasn't to show my face. At 4.30pm, a good hour after school had finished, Woodham appeared at my classroom door and entered smiling broadly.

"It's fine Francis. It was about absolutely nothing. She was just complaining about you not giving Jemima a B plus for her essay, when the toe-rag sitting next to her had got one for more or less the same essay. She felt that Mrs Lee's mark was inaccurate and that Jemima should get a B plus. I explained that you'd given a B grade and that was that. We had a very long discussion about the difference between a B and B plus. So I think for the sake of this one, ignore Mrs Lee's mark, give her B and leave it at that."

I laughed. I couldn't believe that I had got so worried about such a pathetic issue. I would do as Woodham said, stick with my original mark. If the exam board wanted to change it then that was their problem, not mine. All of this worry over the difference between a B and B plus!

"There is another interesting thing, though," Woodham added. "Jemima is getting personal tuition from Mr Morgan, and, although Mrs Killen was insistent that Mr Morgan hadn't looked at the essay, I think he might have put them up to this. But don't worry about it. Go home, make yourself a Martini and forget about it."

"A Martini?"

"Well, a Gibson then," he said. "That's what Cary Grant drank in *North By North West* – or was it *Charade?*"

"Hey, that's my favourite film," I exclaimed.

"Sometimes I feel that the film has many connections with teaching."

BILLY JOHNS AND THE EMOTOPIA

A week before all of this, my experiment with the "E-Notes" had come to an end. Melissa virtually ran the show. She had put all the results onto an amazing spreadsheet, which not only enumerated how many "E-Notes" the pupils in the form had received, but also what they had got them for (she'd had the idea that each recipient should write on the "E-Note" why they had got it).

So for example, a typical pupil's record might read like this:

"Anita Patel: 30 E-Notes: 5 for smiling, 10 for sharing sweets, 5 for carrying bags, 10 for helping with work."

The spreadsheet enabled her to produce a league table of the most helpful students in the class. Weirdly enough, it wasn't the most helpful and co-operative students who were top of the league tables but the most competitive. The league table also confirmed a lot of stereotypes; the boys appeared to have given each other a lot of "E-Notes" for playing football with each other, and the girls for helping each other with reading.

We talked about the findings as a class, and most of them agreed that actually the "E-Notes" made life very uncomfortable because you never quite knew whether someone was helping you because they were being genuinely nice to you, or because they wanted an "E-Note". I hadn't foreseen this; as for my vision that from such an experiment a new "Emotopia" could be built, an alternative to capitalism, I could see now that this was totally unrealistic – such a system would merely create a world even more duplicitous and self-serving than we had at the moment.

But guess who was languishing at the bottom of Melissa's league table? It was Billy Johns, the boy I had given a detention to at the beginning of the year. He had only received 5 "E-Notes" for carrying someone's bag, and this was from Melissa. He was supposed to have been helping her with running the "E-notes" scheme. But she had told me that he had quickly become entangled with arguments with other kids; he'd been very officious about whether their "E-Notes" were genuine or not, and then had given up trying to record who had them.

I could feel that real trouble was brewing for Billy and I was proved right. During my first few months as Billy's form tutor were relatively OK, except that it was clear that he wasn't doing any homework. Notes from teachers had appeared in his Homework Diary – the planner where the pupils had to write down their homework tasks – very regularly. I had talked to Billy about this and a few detentions had been meted out. However, he hadn't bothered turning up to them.

Rather than getting heavy-handed straight away, I had decided on a different tack. I announced to the form group that I would run a "Homework Club" every Tuesday lunchtime and said to Billy that it would be a very good idea for him to come along. And he did. He was happy to work with a few others of his classmates during the lunchtime. He asked me for advice about his History and English – I wasn't his English teacher. I could see that he was struggling to keep up with the work. His spelling wasn't great and he seemed to have a limited understanding of the texts he was studying.

He was beginning to get a sense that he wasn't going to make it; he nearly always seemed to get bad marks, even when he did try. Part of the art of marking is to give a pupil encouragement and confidence, enable them to see where their weaknesses are and try to make them set targets for improvement for their next piece of work. Most of the comments Billy got even when he put some effort in were negative.[10] Despite all of this, he seemed to be coping – well, just about.

But then things started to become more serious. First, Billy bunked off school one day. He'd clearly forged a note from his mum; I phoned home to make further inquiries. His mother confirmed my suspicions.

I was astonished by Billy's reaction when I confronted him with this evidence later. He looked me in the eye and said in a very sincere way that he had been in school. I showed him his own forged note.

"That's just a mistake," he said casually with a brush of his hand. "I was in this dump."

I showed him my register where I had marked him absent. But he was so insistent and sounded so plausible that I felt I had to double-check. Two other teachers confirmed that he had been absent from their lessons.

I then showed all of this evidence to the Head of Year, Jim Saunders. Jim caught up with Billy just before registration and exploded at him. He stood nose to nose with Billy and blasted out in his face, "I know you are lying. Don't you tell me these lies!"

---

[10] Negative marking. After I left Humbards, the school declined very rapidly and was threatened with closure by Ofsted because of the poor behaviour of the children. There were, no doubt, many reasons for this but I would hazard a guess that when the catchment area of the school changed – the school was obliged to take many more students from disadvantaged homes – some of the teachers found it very difficult to adapt. They had been used to teaching able to middling students, and castigating the low achievers. If low achievers are all you have got in a school, and your staff tends to mark negatively, you have a recipe for disaster. Low achievement quickly becomes disaffection.

Billy appeared unmoved. He calmly replied that he had been in school. Every teacher had got it wrong, he was in school. I had to admire Billy here. His solipsism was remarkable: there was only one reality, the reality he invented for himself.

Having shouted very loudly at him and got nowhere, Jim decided to pass the matter back to the Deputy Head of Year, who was the recently appointed Yolanda Williams, my best pal on the staff. Yolanda gave Billy an after-school detention, to which he turned up because his mother had been informed about it.

The following week Billy started to open up to me. He admitted that he *had* bunked off but he had done so because he hated his French lessons. I inquired further about this and found out that there had been quite a bit of trouble going on in these lessons. The French teacher, an affable Parisian man with an easy-going manner, had taken to shouting at Billy because he and a couple of his mates never listened to him and preferred to indulge in toy fights instead.

I arranged a meeting with the French teacher, Mr Fournier and Billy so that we could sort it out. But, before this happened, Billy started saying that he was frightened of Mr Fournier because he was threatening him; he was also grabbing him. He didn't say where but I assumed he meant on his arm. He was a little hesitant in saying this which gave him credibility, because normally he was so strident when he was lying. A couple of his friends also seemed to endorse his version of events. The three of them thought that Mr Fournier's manic shouting and his attempts to touch them were very weird.

Now we were entering dangerous territory; Billy was a proven liar and Mr Fournier just didn't look like the type who would man-handle eleven-year-old boys, except in desperation. I told Yolanda who investigated it further. She talked to some trustworthy girls in the class and found out that the way Billy and his mates were talking about Mr Fournier was totally false. Mr Fournier was a nice teacher who had, on a couple occasions, shouted, with good reason, at the miscreants. There was no suggestion that he was trying to grab the boys.

The meeting between Billy, Yolanda, Mr Fournier, and myself was in many ways hilarious. I could see immediately why Billy had gone after him because his approach was so different from that of most teachers. Yolanda and I were trying to be firm with Billy, and attempted to get him to sign up to a code of behaviour. This included all the obvious things; no calling out, no fighting, finishing homework, putting your hand up.

Mr Fournier was on a different planet. He said in rolling Clouseau-like cadences that he just wanted Billy to be his friend, that he knew in his inner heart Billy was good, so good, he just wanted to reach out to that goodness, to find it, to be friends and so on.

I had to do my best to stop laughing because he was being so French about the whole thing. The no-nonsense Yolanda wasn't impressed at all; Yolanda was from a working class West Indian background that was pretty disciplinarian. For all her trendy clothes and clubbing at the weekends, she ran a tight ship; there was no messing with her in the classroom. By the end of the meeting, we had managed to get Billy to agree to behave.

I talked to Mr Fournier afterwards. He said that in the exclusive French schools where he had taught, relationships between pupils and staff were much warmer. Teachers were more like friends to the pupils.

A few weeks later Mr Fournier asked his supply agency for a transfer to another school in London. He disappeared very abruptly, leaving a fog of rumours behind him; kids said, quite mistakenly, that he'd been sacked for touching up the boys.

Guess who started those rumours?

In the meantime, real trouble was gathering around Billy Johns. When I saw him in the corridor I could almost see the problems buzzing around him in great, black swarms. It seemed that he'd somehow managed to organise a knife fight between two boys – from which he himself had been absent.

He'd set the whole thing up by phone. He had contacted Pavan, an Indian boy – who used to be his friend, but who had fallen out with him because he had refused to let Billy copy up his homework – and told him that his neighbour, who went to another school, was pissed off with Pavan because he thought that Pavan had been dissing him. Billy had then phoned up the neighbour, whom Billy and Pavan knew from primary school, and said more or less the same thing to this boy, Joe. He had conducted a few more phone calls of this nature over the next week, and by the end of it Pavan and Joe were meeting outside the Chinese takeaway with their respective mates.

Joe, who was a much "harder" boy than Pavan, carried a knife. There was a brief fight, with the knife being flashed around. Pavan got slashed across the arm – his sleeve was torn, and blood was drawn – and he had fled before he got properly beaten up; but Pavan's mates and Joe's gang had hung around for a bit, shouting obscenities at each other. The police were called and the crowd dispersed.

The nature of Billy's involvement was only discovered when Yolanda and I investigated. Yolanda phoned the school that Joe attended and said to the Headteacher that Pavan had had to go to hospital with stitches and was now in fear for his life. Parents were then phoned and the truth came out about Billy stirring things up between Pavan and Joe.

I myself got a few worried and irate parents contacting me, saying that they didn't want their children to have anything more to do with Billy. Now the true nature of how Billy was interacting with the other pupils came out: he was bullying them, and using an unholy mixture of bribes, threats of violence and rumour-mongering to keep them under his thumb.

It wasn't an easy situation to sort out because the school's usual method of dealing with difficult kids – that of putting the fear of God into them by shouting at them – just wasn't going to work with Billy. He was a hardened case. He was the tough, stocky son of a massive builder and a supermarket packer. His parents obviously shouted at him regularly; if these presences couldn't intimidate Billy into behaving, we certainly weren't going to be able to control him. I talked to them on the phone but it didn't seem to have much effect.

Later that term, Billy got his interim report. It was appalling; a row of poor marks for behaviour and achievement. He threatened to rip it up in my presence. His attitude towards me, which had always been quite good, had noticeably deteriorated; he frequently ignored me when I spoke to him. There was an equivalent deterioration in his appearance; his uniform was dirty, smeared in food stains and his hair was wild and tangled. Then bits of equipment started going missing in the class: teachers' pencils and pens, kids' PE trainers, coats and bags.

We knew it was Billy but had no evidence. I was forced to

confront him with these suspicions when one parent, the father of Eric Larkin, who was also in the form, phoned up and started threatening to come into school and sort the kid out himself if he didn't get Eric's trainers back. His whole tone scared me. He was clearly a bully himself and wasn't going to let the problem go.

I made some investigations, and managed to get some pupils to say that they had seen Billy in the PE changing rooms – just before the trainers had gone missing. I then found out from Billy himself that he had "borrowed" them and then left them for Eric in the changing rooms. They were never seen again.

I decided to call Billy's Dad. I needed to talk to him about a lot of things: Billy's work, his appearance, the allegations against him.

His Dad lumbered into school. He was a vast man dressed in dirty, paint-spattered overalls; he wore earrings and had a greying skinhead. You might think from his appearance, and his son's behaviour, that he was a thug, but he wasn't at all. Really, he was a very sweet man, who was just trying to hold his life and his family together.

Yolanda and I told him about the list of Billy's crimes and he listened with a grimly clenched jaw. He shook his head disconsolately at Billy who was there in the interview room with us.

"What you got to say to this?" he finally said to Billy.

Billy launched into a volley of adamant denials. His dad shook his head again in an even more lugubrious fashion. He knew all about Billy's compulsive lying. The boy's determined sincerity didn't fool him for one second.

This was partly the problem for Billy. He had lied so much about so many things that, even if he did now tell the truth, no one would believe him.

Yolanda told Mr Johns that she knew Billy was lying. Mr Johns then turned to Billy and said in a resigned fashion, "Now Billy just tell the truth. You nicked those trainers, didn't you? There's no point lying, is there? You know what happens when you lie, you get a whack, don't you? Now you know I never hit you except when you lie, don't you?"

This might sound like a very brutal way of talking to a child, and part of me could see that Mr Johns's parenting skills weren't up to much, but I couldn't help feeling a degree of sympathy.

Billy's lower lip began to quiver. He bunched his hands into fists.

"I ain't done nuffink! I ain't done nuffink! Yer just picking on me!"

"But Billy, you're not facing facts," Yolanda said quietly but insistently. "You are not doing your homework. You are bullying other children. This has to stop. You have to start working.

106

We know you can. We know you can make friends. Do you promise to make an effort?"

Suddenly, Billy burst into tears. His tough-boy face melted into a tiny, frightened child's. "I promise. I promise. I ain't gonna be bad anymore. I ain't gonna. I promise!"

Mr Johns seemed quite moved. He said that things were very difficult at home. He and Mrs Johns were in the process of getting a divorce. His eldest son had been sent away to a youth offenders' institute in Leeds because he had become totally unmanageable. He was having to do a building job in France and was rarely in the country, and he found it difficult to know what to do with Billy. But he agreed to pay the money for the missing trainers.

At the end of the interview, Billy turned to his father, his face drenched in tears and hugged him tightly around the neck. "Oh Daddy, Daddy, take me away from this place. They hate me here. They hate me. Everyone hates me. I have to come with you," he pleaded, leaning into his father's huge, bear-like chest.

Mr Johns cleaned away Billy's tears with a handkerchief and soothed him. It was quite a disturbing scene. I realised that I was on the verge of tears as well. I knew only too well what it was like to be a child in the middle of a bitter divorce. I knew only too well what it was like to watch my father disappear to another country for months on end.

As I staggered out of the interview room, Yolanda asked me whether I was all right. I said that I was fine. I wandered along the corridor in a daze. Now I realised why I had been so disturbed when I had first arrived at the school as a teacher, as long-dormant memories of my eleven-year-old self had resurfaced. I had been a pupil at the school for a few months when I was eleven. The interview with Billy had reminded me of some of the troubles I had negotiated myself. I had been compelled to lie to my mother, telling her that I hated my father and my paternal grandmother because I knew she liked hearing me speak like that. It was a way of stopping my mother being angry with me; perhaps the only way. I had lied and lied to her, and those lies had ripped through the fibres of my soul. They had torn me apart because I had secretly loved my father and my paternal grandmother. I knew only too well what Billy was going through. I understood where his lies came from now.

Despite being so traumatic, the interview was judged a success because the next day Billy came into school with a bounce in his step, a clean uniform and nicely cut hair. He gave me the money for the missing trainers and seemed happier. He also gave me this note on West Ham paper:

To Mr Gilbert and Miss Williams
Sorry for being bad! I have promised to my mum and dad to be

on Excellent behaviour and to tell the truth and have all my
homework in on time.

  Yours Billy Johns.

That note did mark a turning point. Sure, there were still real problems – a repeated failure to hand in homework; fallings out with other people in the form; and one incident when he bashed a kid with a bad back on the base of his spine – supposedly by accident. But in all of these cases – now that I had established contact with the father – I was able to phone the parents up immediately and get the problem sorted before it escalated.

At the end of the academic year, Billy had made some proper friends, improved his work, and had received quite a few merit marks – teachers' commendations – for his improved approach. While he continued to get into trouble, he was surviving.

A BIT ON THE SIDE

Just after the distress of dealing with Billy Johns, Yolanda visited me as I was clearing up in my classroom one lunchtime. She smiled conspiratorially and I smiled back. It felt like the pair of us had, in tackling Billy's problems, entered a labyrinth, a dark place somewhere under the earth, full of twisting corridors, dead ends and scary precipices. It's very difficult to explain this sensation of psychological stress to people who are not teachers. Perhaps this inability to convey the true nature of teaching is why so many teachers marry other teachers – because no one else quite understands.

Yolanda's eyes glinted. She pouted her lips and grinned again. "So how's it going here? Still filing worksheets are we?"

I grinned back. "You know me, if there's a worksheet to file, I'll file it."

"You're too obsessive with that filing cabinet you know. It's very worrying. It seems like that filing cabinet is all you've got in your life."

"Yes. I know, I'm a bit of a sad character."

"I suppose I am too..." Yolanda said, her face suddenly losing its merry, sparkling sheen.

"What do you mean? What's the matter?"

Yolanda sighed. "Oh I don't know, it's just that sometimes life gets a bit tedious. And you need to spice things up a bit."

"What do you mean tedious? I thought all those shenanigans with Billy Johns was pretty interesting," I said, not catching her drift at all.

Yolanda spread out her arms and lifted her chin. Her amazing black hair shone in the light. She looked magnificent.

"That's all well and good, but man cannot live by teaching alone. There's got to be more, hasn't there? I found that at university. You know, you have to do outrageous things every now and then. Live dangerously."

I grinned. "So what dangerous things did you do there?"

"Oh I don't know, just silly things. Once I did it with a guy in a lecture theatre."

Yolanda's eyes expanded and she giggled.

"What!" I exclaimed, not believing what I was hearing. "You… in a lecture theatre? Was anyone else there?"

Yolanda laughed. "No. They'd gone, but it was great anyway."

I blushed. And then laughed a forced laugh. I wasn't quite sure where this conversation was heading.

"Well, that certainly sounds interesting," I said.

"It was. But the guy was a shmuck. Two-timing me."

"No! That's terrible," I said.

She rolled her tongue about her lips. "Oh I don't know. I just seem to keep being second best. I was just his bit on the side. But I don't mind. It was just the way it was."

I was puzzled. I didn't quite know how we had got to this point. In a most forthright, teacherly voice, I asked Yolanda what she meant exactly. Her eyes darted over the ceiling as she repeated, "I'm just used to being a guy's bit on the side."

"Oh come on, Yolanda, you can do better that. You should believe in yourself a bit more," I replied, trying to give her my best words of advice. She agreed, somewhat glumly, and said that she'd see me around.

It was only much later that I realised that her mysterious words might have had something to do with me.

PARENTS FROM HELL?

It started so innocently. There was a note in Melissa's homework diary: "Please could you confirm that the homework timetable in the planner is the correct one." I looked at Melissa in a puzzled fashion during morning registration and asked her why this strange request was in the planner.

She looked up from reading *Mansfield Park*. "Don't ask me," she said. "Nothing to do with me."

I wrote in the planner that it *was* the correct timetable. The next week, when I came to sign the homework planners again, I found another note: "We are very concerned that Melissa is not being set homework according to this schedule. Please advise us about what our next step should be. Mr and Mrs Cruickshank."

I flicked through the planner and saw that the parents had filled in the gaps – in red ink – where homework should have been set and wasn't. They had done a meticulous and scrupulous job; they had gone through the whole year and highlighted that such and such homework had not been allotted on the correct day. They had then pointed out where homework had been "incorrectly" set – i.e. not on the day according to the timetable.

I showed Yolanda the planner in the Lower School office. She blanched. "It's mad. They must have spent hours writing this stuff in."

"What I can't work out is why they didn't highlight this before," I said. "It seems like they've actually enjoyed going through the planner like this."

Yolanda sighed deeply. "I suppose I'll have to phone them."

I caught up with Yolanda at lunch-time. She handed me the planner with a strained face, rolling her eyes. "How did the phone call go?"

"I spoke to Mr Cruickshank and he demanded – not asked, *demanded* – to see all of Melissa's teachers. He is very angry about the lack of homework she's been getting. About her not being stretched," she said.

"She is very bright," I said. "I don't think I've come across such an intelligent eleven-year-old before."

"Yeah, but the man won't listen to reason! I told him that it wasn't possible to have every teacher to speak to him, and that Parents' Evening was coming up. Eventually I got him to agree to meet with me and you tonight."

"What? He's coming in tonight?"

"With Mrs Cruickshank," Yolanda said. "Looking forward to a pleasant evening?"

Yolanda also arranged for a senior teacher to be in attendance. Jim Saunders – the actual Year Head – was away on a school trip, and so the Deputy Head, Mrs Jones, came along. Yolanda and I felt comforted by having Mrs Jones along not only because she was one of the school's big hitters – she had an aura of motherly authority – but also because she knew the Cruickshanks socially. They lived on the same street and were on the same Residents' Association committee.

At the end of the day, the parents, grim-faced in their best clothes, Mr Cruickshank in a charcoal grey pinstripe suit, Mrs Cruickshank in a twin-set and pearls, met Yolanda and me in reception. Without saying much, we escorted them to Mrs Jones' office. I could feel their aggression bristling in the long silence that engulfed us as we headed through the maze-like old school building to the office.

Mrs Jones greeted them affably, calling them by their Christian names, and asked them to sit down. They did so. Mrs Jones remained behind her desk, while Yolanda and I sat with the parents. This had an unfortunate effect because it felt as if we were all being interviewed by Mrs Jones.

Mr Cruickshank produced a notebook and began to read out the homework assignments that had been set for his daughter during the last week: Science was to draw and label a picture of the human heart, Geography to write a "short" paragraph on soil erosion, History to draw a map of the Battle of

Hastings, English to read two chapters of a "simple" teenage novel, and so on.

After he had finished this, he looked up and said: "Mrs Cruickshank and I feel our daughter is not being challenged. She is very clever. It appears her homework consists largely of colouring and drawing."

Mrs Jones leaned back in her chair and smiled. "Miss Williams, any thoughts about this?"

Yolanda was a bit taken aback by this. She'd been expecting Mrs Jones to give a talk at this point.

"I think she is a clever girl and needs to be stretched," she said.

"Because you teach her English, don't you?" Mrs Jones said. "Perhaps that would be the best place to start. If we could put Melissa on an extended reading scheme and attempt to meet her Special Needs that way, it might work."

Yolanda nodded.

"We are particularly worried about Melissa's English. It appears to be deteriorating," Mrs Cruickshank said. "She's starting to come out with some ghastly language. She says 'ain't' regularly now. And 'my God'. She tells me that even certain teachers talk like this!"

Yolanda nodded again. She was beginning to sweat. All eyes were on her. As Melissa's English teacher, she had suddenly become the focus for the aggression.

"And we did notice that Melissa's incorrect usage of the apostrophe is not being corrected in her English book," Mrs Cruickshank continued. "She appears to have forgotten the difference between 'its' and 'it's' in its possessive and contracted form. It really isn't good enough, Mrs Jones!"

"Yes, it is a problem. But I have no doubt that we can solve it. As you have just seen, Miss Williams will provide Melissa with further reading activities. And perhaps Mr Gilbert could co-ordinate with the other teachers and devise a further reading list for the other subjects?" Mrs Jones said. "He is the Study Skills co-ordinator in the school and this is just the kind of thing that he should be doing."

I nodded grimly. This was work. Major work.

Mr and Mrs Cruickshank were very pleased with the outcome of the interview, and reminded Mrs Jones that they would see her at the Residents' Association Barbecue on Saturday. They said their goodbyes curtly to Yolanda and me.

FALLOUT

Yolanda and I decamped to the pub after that. I had a Guinness and Yolanda a lager.

"Fucking hell, I can't believe Jonesy dropped us in the shit like that," Yolanda said after the alcohol had loosened her tongue.

"Did she?"

"Of course she did. She put it all back on to us," Yolanda said. "Now I've got to write a whole reading scheme for Melissa."

"But perhaps she needs it," I said.

"What? Are you taking Jonesy's side on this?" Yolanda said, clearly shocked.

I sipped at my Guinness and considered. "Sure, I don't like the extra work. But when he read out all that homework, it did make you think, didn't it? It was fairly elementary stuff for a kid like Melissa. I mean she's reading *Mansfield Park*."

"But surely the curriculum is Jonesy's area? She's in charge of the curriculum. She should be monitoring the curriculum so that it challenges all the kids," Yolanda said.

I smiled. "That's not Jonesy's area. It's the government's area. The National Curriculum is set by central government. Jones had no more control over it than a road sweeper. It's a one-size-fits-all system."[11]

Our conversation then degenerated in a hideous slagging off of the Tory government, which we both loathed for similar and differing reasons. The alcohol helped give us the illusion

---

[11] *National Curriculum, National Disaster?* In his book of the same name, Rhys Griffith argues that the National Curriculum, which was introduced in 1989, has failed to challenge pupils of all abilities. His diary of watching numerous lessons is persuasive. By putting an emphasis on teaching subjects separately, and somewhat arbitrarily assigning certain subjects to be taught, the curriculum has meant that pupils do not join the dots between the subjects areas and nothing feels significant.

that all our criticisms would somehow make a difference.

They didn't.

Melissa became a test case for me. On the computer, I had designed a pro-forma for an Individual Action Plan. In essence, it was a very simple thing; just a list of targets to be met over the coming months. Luckily, I found her Science teacher sympathetic and she came up with a clever catch-all book for her to read: *On the Origin Of Species* by Darwin. It embraced geography, history, biology and philosophy.

Melissa Cruickshank – An Individual Action Plan

1. In English, Melissa will read all of Jane Austen's novels and write reviews for each one. To be completed by December.
2. She will also read *On the Origin of Species* by Charles Darwin and complete exercises set by her Science teacher.
To be completed by June.

However, we hadn't banked upon Melissa herself. Just before registration in the morning, on a rather wet June day, two girls from the tutor group approached me. Normally they were simpering, giggly girls but today they were in a more sombre mood.

"Oh sir, I'm not being funny or anything but we need to talk to you," Tracey King said, looking at me as though I was bound to find anything she said funny. She was the class joker

118

and, while she drove half the staff insane, I found her hilarious – although I knew I shouldn't.

I guided Tracey and her friend, Catherine, into our form base and listened to their story.

"Well, sir, it's Melissa. We found her in the dinner hall just now and she was crying!" Tracey said.

"Go on," I said to Tracey.

"Well, sir, you know that Melissa was off on Tuesday, don-cha?'

I nodded. She had given me a note from her mother saying that she was ill.

"She tried to commit suicide on that day, that's why she wasn't in," Catherine blurted out, clearly frustrated that Tracey was taking too long to tell me the story.

Catherine then told me that Melissa was saying that she hated her life, and that she had no friends, and that she wanted to die. Tracey added that Melissa's mother pinched and slapped her.

Apparently, Melissa had tried to kill herself by swallowing some pills. I didn't know what to say to the girls; this kind of thing didn't crop up that regularly. I thanked the girls for telling me and later took the register, ruminating upon the problem. I scrutinised Melissa, who was sitting at the front of the room reading *Pride and Prejudice*. No one was sitting next to her. But then again, no one really ever did. She did look pale. And then I reflected that since the day her parents had come into school, she had become more and more withdrawn. Her face was pale, and she seemed painfully thin. I should have seen it before, but now it seemed obvious to me that something was wrong.

I thought about asking Melissa about it but decided against this; I needed to speak to Mrs Jones before listening to what Melissa had to say. We had been given quite clear instructions that if we ever heard of any serious problem we should report it to the Deputy Head. He would then log it in a file and get in touch with Social Services if need be.

After a bit of running around, going from office to staffroom, back to the office, and then back to the staffroom, I got hold of Yolanda who was just as concerned as I was when she heard the story. She questioned Catherine and Tracey further; they told her what they had told me. They weren't lying or stirring anything up.

It was time to talk to Melissa. Luckily, we caught her coming out of the form room. However, we didn't have much time. Both of us were teaching next lesson, and Melissa had lessons to go to. The timetable grinds remorselessly on, even in the face of suicide and death. Perhaps that's what I find so comforting about schools; everything is so regimented, so definitively timetabled and pigeon-holed, that suffering has to take a back seat. There are always other things to distract you from the real horrors of life; the entirely invented horrors of the curriculum are not nearly as bad as reality.

We had to ask Melissa about her welfare in hurried, whispered tones in a busy corridor, with lots of other kids milling by.

"So, you're not too happy at the moment?" Yolanda asked.

Melissa nodded almost imperceptibly, but she did nod. Tears were welling up in her eyes.

"What's the matter?"

"I... I...," Melissa said, the tears now dropping to the floor.

The bell rang for lesson time to start; we were directly underneath it and it shuddered through us. It was five past nine; a whole day's worth of lessons to get through and already I felt drained. But Melissa felt worse, a lot, lot worse. That much was clear.

I suppose we could have asked Melissa to come down to the medical room right there and then, but we didn't. Lessons beckoned. I asked Melissa to go; now was not the time to talk. Tracey and Catherine, who had been hovering behind us, swept up and started to talk to Melissa. The three of them walked slowly along the corridor, leaving us to quickly confer.

Yolanda decided that she would phone Mrs Cruickshank and ask her whether the absence note she had written was correct.

Yolanda got back to me at lunch-time and said that the

mother denied all knowledge of Melissa attempting suicide and that she thought Melissa was lying. Yolanda was clearly shocked by the mother's lack of concern or sympathy.

We decided that we needed to talk to Melissa again, and hear directly from her whether the story was true. We rooted her out from the dining hall just after lunch, before afternoon registration.

Yolanda said to Melissa that we wanted to talk to her; and she followed us hesitantly to the interview room. It was a new, purpose-built room and, to my mind, it looked incredibly impersonal; it was more like a police interrogation chamber than somewhere to have a friendly chat. I asked Melissa whether she wanted anyone with her. Melissa snatched at this opportunity and said that she wanted Catherine by her side.

Yolanda wasn't happy. She hummed and hawed about having Catherine there; she would spread rumours about Melissa if anything really bad was revealed. To my mind, Melissa had already said the worst to Catherine, and it was obvious that Melissa wanted her there.

But I didn't want to argue with Yolanda and said that I didn't mind either way. Yolanda didn't know what to do. Eventually, after a bit more backing and forthing between the pair of us, we called Catherine in.

We began by asking how Melissa felt she was getting on at school.

"I've got no friends," she mumbled.

We were able to reassure her because the mere fact Catherine was there showed she had friends. Then we asked gently about how she was getting on at home. Melissa claimed none of her friends phoned her up when she was at home. I said that my friends rarely phoned me up when I was at home; I had to do a lot of running in that regard.

Yolanda pounced on this and repeated what I had said: "Mr Gilbert's friends don't phone him up. Sometimes we have to make an effort with friends!"

While this made me sound like a sad case, it had the desired effect. She brightened a little. Then her face fell. Without looking at us, she said: "I hate it at home."

There was another pause.

I asked her what had happened on Tuesday.

Pause.

And suddenly: "I tried to kill myself," she blurted out.

"But why?" I asked. "Are we putting too much pressure upon you with all these extra reading schemes?"

Melissa didn't answer. Then she insisted that we mustn't tell her parents because they would be angry with her. She then added that once, when she went away with the school on holiday, she had written a postcard to her parents saying that she missed them, but this was a lie. She hadn't missed them at all. The only people she had were her friends. "I just want to be with my friends. I don't care about my family. I can talk to my friends," she said, looking at Catherine as she said this.

I piped up that that was good, very good. Talking to people was brilliant.

Wrong thing to say in Yolanda's view, who interrupted me in mid-flow and said that she thought it would wise for Melissa not to talk too much about all of this. I back-tracked, feeling chastened, and said that Miss Williams was quite right. Don't talk too much.

After the interview, I apologised for saying this. I explained that when I was Melissa's age, I had endured a pretty difficult time at home and had found talking to people helped. Yolanda said that was fine but unfortunately she had dealt with a girl who had told other pupils lots of lurid stories about slashing her wrists and managed to scare them witless.

Yolanda had dealt with parents complaining about the gruesome tales of self-harm that their children were being subjected to. This struck me as a cowardly argument but I didn't say anything. She seemed pretty tense and she had a nasty cough. Now was not the time to argue with her.

Yolanda and I descended the stairs and caught Mrs Jones, the Deputy Head, in her office. Rather surprisingly, she didn't appear shocked at all that there was evidence that her friends were cruel parents. She sighed. "Ah, I feared something like this might happen," she said. "And much sooner than I had thought. Melissa is still very young to get rebellious like this."

"That's what it is, is it? Rebelliousness?" I asked.

"When you have daughters of your own, you'll learn what they are like. Especially if they are bright. They don't take out their aggression upon other people like boys do. It all turns inward," Mrs Jones said. "Terrible things can happen. They become overwhelmed with the meaninglessness of everything and yet remain intensely competitive, seeking rewards in producing perfect work."

We talked a bit more about the programme of study Melissa had been on. She had, according to her teachers, been doing it brilliantly. They were astonished that a child could read *On the Origin of Species* so quickly and produce such an amazing analysis of it.

Again, Mrs Jones sighed. "She hasn't got a childhood, has she?"

"Perhaps we brought this upon her?" I ventured, feeling guilty that we had drawn up such a demanding programme.

"No, it would have happened without the programme. The child doesn't know what it is like to be young and silly and muck around. Poor girl."

Mrs Jones picked up the phone and called Mr Cruickshank at work. I could tell that he was quite belligerent because Mrs Jones was exceptionally diplomatic.

"We just need to clear up a few things, Philip," Mrs Jones

said. "Melissa appears upset... No, I don't want to go through what she has said now... I'd like to see you today or tomorrow if possible. We need to sort this out quickly."

Once again, Yolanda and I met Mr and Mrs Cruickshank at reception after school, and guided them to Mrs Jones' office. They appeared much more unhappy than they had been before. Mr Cruickshank was particularly bullish. "What nonsense has Melissa been saying?" he demanded. Yolanda said that we would talk about it in Mrs Jones's office.

This time Mrs Jones was not sitting behind her desk, but had drawn up her seat next to Melissa in the centre of the office. The other chairs were arranged in a circle. I noticed that Mrs Jones only said a brief hello to her friends without the civilities of before.

Almost as soon as he had sat down Mr Cruickshank barked: "What is this rubbish you have been telling everyone, Melissa?"

Melissa's head remained bowed. She didn't say anything. She appeared frightened, but there was something in her body language, her hunched position, that indicated that she was defiant. I felt like telling Mr Cruickshank that he was bullying his child.

"Now then, Philip, I think we just want to sort out the confusion over this," Mrs Jones said calmly. She held Melissa's hand and said, "Melissa perhaps you would like to say again

126

what you told me earlier. There's nothing to be afraid of. Your parents love you, and we all want what is best for you, don't we?"

Her tone and approach was brilliant. The two parents could not disagree with her, and yet she was implicitly admonishing them for being uncaring.

Mrs Jones repeated her previous comment; this time giving Melissa a cuddle. The girl looked up and wiped the tears from her eyes.

"I tried to swallow those pills. I thought they would kill me. They didn't. They didn't work."

"Now we are all glad that they didn't! Aren't we?" Mrs Jones said with a laugh of relief. "Because we all want you to be happy. Your parents just want you to be happy. Now it occurred to me that you might be finding all this extra work too much."

Mr Cruickshank was about to interrupt. He was shaking his head. But Mrs Jones stopped him by holding up her hand.

"I would like to invite my friends over. I don't want to be studying every night. I want to watch TV! I'm sick of all this work! I just want to be like everyone else," she said.

"Well, perhaps that's a good idea for now. You can always go back to it when you are ready. And I am sure that your parents would welcome your friends to come over," Mrs Jones said, with a sympathetic smile at the parents.

Reluctantly, they nodded their heads. I could see something incredible happening. Mrs Jones's natural sympathy for Melissa was beginning to seep into their stony hearts. They were beginning to see that they had been looking at things the wrong way round. They left the interview in silence. Mrs Cruickshank took Melissa's hand gingerly, almost diffidently.

I was quite anxious about how Melissa might be feeling the next day after that interview but she seemed relatively calm. She smiled gently as her friends buzzed around her, and she even made a little joke with me about me forgetting to do the register properly.

Yolanda was bemused by the change. "Do you think she just likes the fact that all these people seem to care about her?"

I agreed, but also told her that I thought that the Cruickshanks now knew we were scrutinising them. They were clearly people who liked to keep up appearances. They had to keep Melissa happy in order to stop the awkward questions.

Perhaps this was the reason. I was never sure. Melissa was a mysterious child – brilliant but fragile. The more I got to know her, I realised that her moods fluctuated a great deal. She could be extremely lively and bubbly one day, but very depressed the next. Over the next few months she seemed to dip in and out of depression, but she never, as far as I was aware, "attempted suicide" again.

YOLANDA IN HOSPITAL

The whole business with the Cruickshanks wore Yolanda out. This fiddly, time-consuming matter came on top of many other commitments.

She had two Year 11 classes – which meant that she had to mark and supervise 60 coursework folders as well as prepare the students for an arduous set of exams. She also had her duties as an Assistant Head of Year which she took very seriously. Often she stayed at school until 6 or 7pm. I seemed to have developed the ability to switch off after work, to go home and throw myself in front of the television and not think about it, but this wasn't the case with Yolanda.

And it was beginning to show. Her eyes looked drawn, and she had developed a hacking cough which she wasn't able to shake off. But she wouldn't take any time off work, despite having obtained a doctor's note: something which she flourished before me like it was a badge of her toughness.

"Hey, you're not Doc Holliday you know," I said to her. "You should stay in bed a few days. You look rough."

"Thanks a lot. I know where to come to for a compliment next time. Anyway, who the fuck is Doc Holliday?"

"He's the gunslinger in *The Gunfight at the OK Corral* who has TB. He's always coughing, but he carries on shooting the bad guys because a guy's gotta do what a guy's gotta do. Or something like that," I said.

"You watch too many films. You should get out more," she replied, and then broke into another cough.

A few days later, Mr Woodham informed us that Yolanda had been admitted to hospital with pneumonia. She'd collapsed over the weekend in her flat. Luckily, her mum had called by on the off-chance, and found her, otherwise it could have been serious.

I visited her the next day in the local hospital. She looked terrible: her mouth was covered in sores and she was painfully thin. Almost emaciated.

"I guess I don't need that fucking Slimfast anymore," she said slowly. Her gums were white. I wasn't quite sure why and didn't ask. I gave her a few audio tapes to listen to and talked a little bit about the gossip at school.

***

I felt angry. Angry that the system had reduced her to such a poorly state. She was exhausted. Completely and utterly overworked. It was only the plodders like me that survived. I wasn't as conscientious as Yolanda. I didn't mark my pupils' work with such diligence, I tossed a lot of paperwork in the bin, I would often improvise lessons without planning in massive detail. Yolanda did things the way Ofsted and all the manuals said you should. Look where it had got her.

A POSITION OF RESPONSIBILITY

"So you're telling me that I need to provide lessons on Study Skills for the sixth form?" I asked Mrs Jones.

"Yes, exactly that," she said with a cherubic smile. She leant back in her chair, luxuriating in the spaciousness of her office.

"But there are no teachers to do it with. I mean it's not a timetabled lesson," I replied.

"Ah, I see what you mean. Well, we were envisaging that you would suspend sixth form lessons for an afternoon, say, every month and get an outside speaker in," she said quickly.

I swallowed hard. Until now, I hadn't quite realised how difficult the job of Study Skills co-ordinator was going to be. I would have to find outside speakers to deliver talks about study skills, or give them myself, to nearly 120 sixth formers. And I only had £1000 in the budget.

But I didn't complain. I didn't even make a fuss. I nodded demurely to Mrs Jones and said that I would do my best.

And I did. I had been given a desk in Morgan's office and a

phone to use. I cleared a space at the very back of the office, tipping the piles of books, boots and bags underneath his desk. I decided that I would be very tidy; I had a tray for papers, a notepad and a telephone. It was a bit awkward sharing an office with Morgan, but since we had both decided that we weren't going to speak to each other, life was somewhat simplified. We didn't have to exchange strained pleasantries. He had his section of the office – which was most of it – and I had my desk.

My final master-stroke was to track down a Personal Digital Assistant in a Dixons one weekend. Morgan may have had his walking sticks, other teachers had their handbags, their knitting, their clipboards and their briefcases, but I had my PDA!

I would produce it at every opportunity – in meetings, in the class, in the corridor, at lunch, at staff-meetings – and show the world that I was no ordinary teacher, I was a techno-wizard, PDA-possessing, educational super teacher.

I was, in fact, an educational super-creep. I actually started reading the *Times Education Supplement* properly, logging down the latest information in my PDA. I babbled the most up-to-date jargon to my colleagues and my wife at home. I had teaching manuals as my bedside reading. I lived, breathed, and ate teacher talk. (I was unbearable!)

I was able to log all my telephone numbers, write my diary,

write memos, lesson plans and insert my results onto it. It was great! And it really helped me with the organisational nightmare of arranging speakers to come into school, and taking the sixth form "off timetable" in order to learn about study skills.

Over the next couple of years, I did manage to get quite a few speakers to come and talk about the right ways to study – by taking notes, writing revision timetables, skim-reading, devising mind-maps and so on – and, on the whole, these talks were reasonably successful. For the most part, the students did listen and some found the lectures useful.

But there were two major problems. Firstly, the speaker was nearly always addressing a hundred kids or so, and secondly, taking the kids "off-timetable" caused huge resentment among the staff.

Inevitable comparisons with Mr Morgan arose.

The worst person to complain was the sixth form Tutor and Head of Practical Engineering, Kelvin Hacker. Hacker was a middle-aged man with a shaved head, earrings and a highly aggressive, if rather camp manner. During tutor sessions I had to visit the tutors, and give out notices about my latest "Study Skills" lessons.

"Old Morgan didn't bother with this rubbish! He just took the kids away on holiday. Why can't you do that?" Hacker spat at me.

The kids in the tutor group, several heavily-made-up girls and three well-dressed, handsome boys, sniggered. Hacker clearly enjoyed playing up to them by giving me an earful.

"I haven't been asked to do that. That's not in my job description," I said.

"Bugger your job description! I mean what is this? Mind-crapping? What's that? Is that when you crap out of your mind? I mean, you must know a lot about that!"

Astonishingly, I never reported Hacker for talking like this. Perhaps it was because I knew he had some close friends on the senior management, or perhaps it was because of the raucous way his tutor group fell about laughing, or perhaps it was because I felt guilty, deep down, about "taking Morgan's job" and felt this was my punishment.

Unfortunately, I had set a poor precedent – from then on Hacker always had a go at me whenever I entered his tutor room. I would just smile weakly and not say anything.

My woes were compounded when I was asked to introduce "Action Planning" in the sixth form; this was an idea whereby students would set themselves targets which were SMART: Specific, Measurable, Achievable, Realistic and Time-related. In other words, they would be encouraged to set themselves some realistic goals in order to improve their work.

HOW TO GENERATE LOTS OF USELESS BITS OF PAPER THAT GET THROWN IN THE BIN

1. Ask that every student becomes an Action Planner.
2. Ask a very junior member of staff, who has inadvertently alienated just about everyone, who knows nothing about Action Planning, and who has no training in the field, to introduce Action Planning.
3. Make sure that nobody really knows what Action Planning *is*, but get people to say it a lot, because it is something that MUST be done.
4. Allow your junior member of staff to come up with a worksheet, saying Individual Action Plan at the top of it, and watch him put this worksheet in every register.
5. Do not give him any time to explain this worksheet to the staff.
6. Let him give a long talk about the worksheet to the sixth form, and make sure none of the students or staff listen to it.
7. Ask the pupils to fill in the Action Plan.
8. Finally, watch those pupils leave those bits of paper in the classroom so that the cleaner can toss them in the bin.

THE SAD TRUTH ABOUT ACTION PLANS

Written Action Plans are a great idea. In theory. John Major and Tony Blair's governments lived off the Action Plan culture during the 1990s. In an Action Plan culture, specific targets and deadlines are set. They are then reviewed later on to see if the targets have been met.

The basic concept in a school environment is that pupils should reflect upon their progress. This is difficult because, if the targets are unclear or unrealistic, the net result is that the pupils become either confused or demotivated.

Jemima Killen's Action Plan

Subject: English Literature
Target: To learn how to analyse an author's use of language
Deadline and evaluation: By February

Subject: Geography
Target: To improve my grades from a C to a B
Deadline and evaluation: By September

Subject: Sociology
Target: To learn how society works
Deadline and evaluation: By Christmas

Subject: Study Skills

Target: To learn how to Mindmap™
Deadline and evaluation: By August

Extra-curricular: To become a great actress
Deadline and evaluation: By next year

Jemima's Action Plan was typical of many of the Action Plans; it contained some reasonable targets. The ones for English Literature and Study Skills were alright because they were SMART: there was something specific that she had to achieve, it was realistic, and there was a clear deadline. The Geography target was typical of a lot of targets that pupils make for themselves; to raise their grades. Unfortunately, there was no specific action she could take to implement this. I tried to explain to the sixth form that they shouldn't do this, but should ask their subject staff for something definite that they could do to improve their work, but it was useless. Lots of Action Plans were similarly flawed. Also, there was a lot of silliness; targets to improve alcohol intake, sex life, and such-like.

CONGRATULATIONS

Although I was quite dispirited about the poor reception that my Action Planning worksheets had received, I soon got over my depression when I realised that the really important people in the school were hugely impressed by my efforts.

The Headteacher and the Deputy Head, Mrs Jones, thought I had done a terrific job. They had been given a target by the governing body to introduce Action Planning into the sixth form by such and such a date, and they could now tick that off in their review.

It was congrats all round.

A PROMOTION TOO FAR

I was hungry for power now. I began to think that the higher up the pecking order you went, the less stress you had to suffer. I saw how powerful people like the Headteacher and Mrs Jones were; they had effectively removed Morgan from his job, they enjoyed great respect (and loathing) throughout the school; they always had smiles on their faces; they had no arduous teaching commitments – except the ones they wanted, plus huge offices and double my wages. And they weren't that old either: in their late thirties – early forties maybe. I estimated that if I moved quickly up the food chain, I might be a Deputy Head or Head in less than ten years.

I could see that if I remained where I was I would just get shat upon, blamed for things that were out of my control, and asked to do far too much work. So, when Mr Woodham approached me and said that he was thinking of removing the Second-in-Department in English from her job and getting someone decent to run the lower school English department, I thought he was giving me the nod to go for it. The Second-in-Department, Mrs Bernard, was an honourable but disheartened woman.

She still enjoyed great authority, but years and years at the school, stuck in a relatively lowly position, had taken their toll. She was prematurely grey, her face was very pale and her classroom had the fustiness of an abandoned library. Great swathes of dusty papers spilled out of her desk, folders were strewn haphazardly across the top of her filing cabinet and the odd mouldy cup of tea or confiscated catapult could be found underneath the detritus. She didn't like any of the senior management but was great friends with Mr Morgan.

Shortly after the Head's comments to me, a whispering campaign started against Mrs Bernard. In the staffroom, Mrs Lee clucked over her knitting that there appeared to be no schemes of work for the lower school, and that the teaching methods were far too traditional. "Time for some young blood, I feel," she said in a loud voice to Grace Malmesbury.

A few days later, a notice was posted – because Mrs Bernard was now in charge of stock, there was an opening for a new person as Second-in-Department. The rest of the department were annoyed about this because they felt that Mrs Bernard was unfairly being fingered for the department's shortcomings, when much of the blame should have fallen on Mrs Lee's shoulders. Yolanda, Mr Morgan, and two other English `teachers had no affection for Mrs Lee, who had managed to piss off everyone with her criticisms of their grammar. Because I was friendly with Yolanda, I was dragooned into being part of a delegation that went to see the Headteacher to explain this. It was a foolish move on my part. The delegation looked terrible; the department huffed and puffed into the Head's room. He looked quite startled when we started blaming Mrs Lee for everything.

By trying to keep everyone happy, I pleased no one. The Head didn't like me for looking like I was trying to scupper his scheme; the rest of the department were quite suspicious of my friendship with him; Mrs Bernard hated me because I had taken Mr Morgan's job; and my Head of Department had begun to detest me when she learned that I was part of the delegation.

And then I made matters even worse by applying for Mrs Bernard's job.

My reasoning was that the Headteacher wanted me to do so, that I should try and get on as quickly as I could and get into a position of real power. I got an interview but failed to get the post. I spouted so much jargon in the interview that the parent governor present didn't know what I was talking about. My fluent patter about introducing "differentiation", "addressing SMART targets within the department", "moving to a modular system", "thinking vertically about ability" even confused Woodham. Only the Local Authority Advisor, himself a great purveyor of jargon, seemed impressed.

No one was appointed. It was a fiasco all round. Mrs Bernard went off sick at about the time of the interviews and then returned to find that she was still Acting Second-in-Department. If her morale had been low before, now it was languishing somewhere in the pits of hell.

EDUCATIONAL SUPER CREEP

What a slick operator I was! I spoke the lingo, I spouted about targets and differentiation, about modular courses and empowering students. I gossiped about other teachers' incompetence, and laughed at their mistakes. I was not a sympathetic figure.

As a result I had got myself widely disliked. The Headteacher kept me at a distance, I was no longer his confidante; he wanted to me to keep doing the sixth form job. I was doing it too well. He was saving thousands of pounds because I was so energetically getting outside speakers to talk to the sixth form.

Even Yolanda was not so close to me. She had a boyfriend now, and I was finding that it was impossible to talk to her, even in the pub on Friday afternoons.

I knew that things were *really* going wrong when the Head joked with me: "Oh Francis, you're such a teacher. I see you walking around and I think you're exactly what a teacher should be; you've got the walk and the talk. You've even got the PDA!"

There was more than a hint of irony in his voice.

TIME TO MOVE ON

My disappointment at my failure to get the Second-in-Department job drove me to look for other jobs almost immediately. After the initial euphoria of having escaped from Tower Hamlets, it now felt unnerving to be teaching in a school where I had once been a pupil. It felt like I hadn't really progressed. I had simply returned to the place where I had been an unhappy eleven-year-old.

I had expected to apply for a lots of jobs. When I was teaching in Tower Hamlets I had had numerous rejections before even getting an interview. This time, however, I was immediately given interviews, and got the first job I went for.

***

I liked the general atmosphere of the Brokers' Boys and Girls' Academy of Excellence in a suburb of South London. Mr

Henry Pullum, the Curriculum Team Leader for the Arts – this school was too trendy for Heads of Departments – was very friendly and the school looked very welcoming on that summer's day. The sun shone on pleasant, airy classrooms. All the students seemed polite and friendly. All in all the school seemed very like Humbards only better: it got better results, it had better resources, and better staff.

Mr Pullum listened sympathetically to my complaints about Morgan and my current position and no one asked me any difficult questions in the interview. I had the job at the end of the day. It was so easy! Too easy, and too fast. A couple of weeks ago, I had been trotting along merrily at Humbards, thinking I would stay for years. Now I only had to get through to the end of the term.

ALLEGATIONS AND JOKES

A couple of days later I was sitting in the Humbards staffroom, reading the newspaper, when Kelvin Hacker crept up behind me. I started fiddling with the newspaper, feeling distinctly uneasy about being in the same room as the one person who consistently tormented me; I could see in the corner of my eye that he was grinning.

He positioned himself against the radiator situated in front of the table where I had been reading until he interrupted me.

"So you're leaving," he said, letting his words taper off into the thin, stale air of the staffroom.

"Yes," I said, looking down at the newspaper.

"Don't you feel you're betraying the school by doing that?" Hacker said, still smiling.

A couple of staff had already asked me this question in a jokey way; I was prepared for it now.

"No," I said coldly.

"Well, I think you are," said Hacker. "And in fact I'm thinking of getting my revenge on you..."

Again he let his words hang in the air. By this time I was severely disturbed. I wrinkled my forehead, and stooped to look at the newspaper in more detail. I didn't want to be hearing this and I didn't know how to respond to it. I pretended I hadn't heard what he said.

"Did you hear what I just said?" Hacker persisted. "I'm thinking of getting my revenge on you, I think that I might get that little squirt Billy Johns to make up some things about you..."

The feeling of humiliation, of powerlessness, was getting worse but I didn't know how to answer. I stayed silent.

"You didn't hear what I said, did you?" Hacker said.

I mumbled something about having to do some marking and got up and left. Walking along the corridor, anger began to well up in me. I had to deal with this somehow. I couldn't have Hacker threatening me like this.

I went to Hacker's immediate boss, the head of sixth form, and told her the story in whispered tones in her office. She nodded and said that Hacker was just like that, adding: "He's just a bit mad really."

Later on during the day, just before a parents' evening, I caught up with Hacker in the corridor and told him that I didn't like what he had said. Finally I had stood up to him! But he was completely unphased and dismissed me with a wave of his hand: "It was just a joke, Gilbert. Don't get worked up about it."

"It didn't feel like a joke," I said.

"It was. It was just me entering the realms of fantasy," he said with a sly smile.

That evening, I talked to the parents of my Year 7 pupils – eleven-year-olds – with a knot in my stomach.

When I finally got home late that evening, my wife persuaded me to phone my union rep. He advised me to take the matter to my Headteacher.

Woodham was sympathetic but also rather cagey. "Look, Francis, I'm sorry he's been making your life difficult. I'll speak to him and see if we can sort it out."

Woodham did speak to Hacker, and while he didn't apologise for his behaviour, he at least acknowledged that his 'pranks' could be misinterpreted. When I passed him in the corridor after his chat with Woodham, he grumbled at me, "Here comes the man with a great sense of humour."

However, his comments ceased. And all the stuff about me teaching the children "Mindcrapping", and "getting his revenge upon me" was dropped.

IN THE PARK

Some of the pupils covered their faces with their hands as I asked, yet again, where Will Jenkins and Albert Tench were. I hadn't seen them in my lesson for the past week, and yet I was sure that I had seen them in school.

When I had taught this class in Year 9, I had been relieved not to have them around; I had been plagued for a few months by the grotesque faces that they kept pulling as they talked to me. At that point, in the mid-1990s, the films of Jim Carrey were popular. The actor specialised in contorting his face into the most stupid positions; his particular favourite was protruding his upper lip to an absurd degree, and twisting his lower lip into a knot of flesh. It was not sophisticated humour and perhaps this was why Jenkins and Tench enjoyed imitating it so much. Every time I called out their names or spoke to them, they would pull this ridiculous face. The class would hoot with laughter, and I would consider my options: send them On Call, ask them to stop, or pretend that nothing was happening. I decided to ignore them, refusing to laugh; and then send them On Call if they did anything else naughty.

Over the next few years – it really did take me two years to adjust to them![12] – I had begun to relax. I actually began to find their antics funny. It became light relief from trudging through the tedium of the English National Curriculum in Year 11.

We developed a "modus vivendi"[13]. Jenkins and Tench would entertain us with their stupid faces, we would laugh at them, and then the rest of the class would get on with the work. Jenkins and Tench, while never doing very much, would not fight the other kids, flick rubber bands across the room, or cuss the teacher. So in a way, the class and I actually missed them when they weren't around that week.

"Where are they then?" I asked, peering deep into the eyes

---

[12] <u>Teachers who do their time.</u> If a school is going to be a successful, happy one, it has to hold onto its staff so that the pupils are not having a different teacher every other week. Children need that emotional stability. The most pernicious thing in an unsuccessful school is the high turn-over of staff.

[13] <u>"Modus Vivendi".</u> I believe this is the most vital concept that any teacher should learn about how to get on with difficult classes. Develop a "modus vivendi" – a way of living with them; give them trade offs, play the rogue with them, make it clear if they are basically OK with you, you will forgive certain misdemeanours. Enter a secret pact with them that enables you and them to get on. Break the rules if necessary, but make sure that you and they are on "friendly terms" day in, day out. This is different from being their friend. Friendly terms means having laugh with the kids, admitting that it's bloody tough teaching them, but you and they should have a little bit of fun. All the teachers who endure, except the fiercest, do this. They never teach you this stuff in Teacher Training College because none of the tutors there have stuck it out in the classroom.

of the class. This was part of the "modus vivendi"; they may not have been the best behaved group in the world but they were truthful with me – about whether they had done the homework, about whether they understood what the hell Shakespeare was on about, and about what the naughty kids were up to in the class.

There was some hushed, excited chatter, and a few kids in the class offered their explanations: "They're in the park!"

"They're in the park and they're smoking!"

"They're in the park and they're doing smack!"

"They're in the park and they're on crack!"

"They're in the park and they're shagging!"

"Year 10 girls!"

"Each other!"

"Trees!"

"All right, all right! That's enough!" I yelled. The ad-lib comments were now raising the class to the pitch of hysterical laughter. "I take it, that whatever they might be doing, they are in the park!"

Everyone nodded. We got on with the lesson, and then, at lunch-time, I ventured out of the staff-room and into the park. Now, to understand fully the implications of what I did here, you have to realise that I was breaking a number of unwritten rules. Like many teachers I am a creature of habit, I follow set rituals every break-time and lunch-time. At break I always have a cup of tea, look in my pigeon hole, wander around the staff-room, check the noticeboards, listen to gossip, and talk to the English Department. At lunch-time I always retire to the staff-room, and read the paper while having my packed lunch – looking up every now and then to join in any relevant moaning.

But today, I took my sandwich with me and walked into the park. Perhaps I was feeling reckless because I was going to be leaving. I hadn't had a stroll in the park since starting at the school – the truth is it reminded me of my childhood too much; I had walked through it to get to school when I was a pupil at the school. I had felt frightened then. Worried that I would get into trouble at home, get into trouble at school, get bullied; the world intimidated me, and that park did too. I had heard lots of grisly rumours about the nasty men that hung out there. I would always run through it at top speed.

I now felt completely liberated. The sun was shining through the oak and elm trees, their branches were swaying gently in the breeze, and the smells from the long grasses were sweet. I believed I had triumphed; I had gone back to the school of my childhood, I had done well there, but I had also got out just in time. I was going to a better job – where I would become a really successful teacher!

These thoughts fluttered through my brain as I turned the corner, and found Tench and Jenkins in the glade where the pupils had told me they would be. Before me was a long stretch of smoothed-down grass, where Tench and Jenkins were busy. They weren't taking drugs, or smoking, or shagging, but playing what looked like bowls. I scanned the scene: they had left a football, their bikes and school bags by a large oak tree, and had made a long runway. Tench was in the process of chucking a black ball down the runway towards a cluster of other balls when he stopped, having registered the look on Jenkins' face.

"Oi, sir, what are you doing here?" Jenkins smiled. He seemed totally unconcerned by my arrival. Or at least he was making a very good job of seeming this way.

"I thought I would find out what you were doing while you are supposed to be in school," I said. I was smiling. I didn't feel that censorious. I was in too much of a good mood.

Jenkins dropped the ball he was holding and headed towards me but Tench held back, pulling one of his customary Jim Carrey faces.

"Look sir, we're just having a little break at lunchtime," he said. "That's all. You can't tell us off for that."

His tone was defensive. Behind his nonchalant swagger, he was worried. His mother was the Headmistress of a primary school, and was insistent with me at Parents' Evenings that Will should get top grades. She was very keen to get him into the sixth form.

"Where were you in my lesson today?" I asked.

"We were there," Tench shouted out.

"I didn't see you there," I replied, putting my hands on my hips.

"We were invisible," Jenkins retorted quickly. "We've been working on this special serum that makes us invisible."

"And I suppose this is the same serum that gets you to pass your GCSEs, which you are taking in a few weeks, without having done any work, or going to any lessons?"

"Yeah, that's the one," Jenkins said. He tapped his pocket. "I've got it right here."

I sniffed the air. How was I going to resolve this one?

"I think your mother wouldn't be very happy to find out you were here," I said.

Jenkins didn't reply but kicked the ground. Yes, he was still frightened of her, despite being a great big teenager.

"So you've been playing bowls here? Is that what you're up to?" I asked.

Jenkins brightened at this. "Yeah, yeah! Do you want a go? It's a great game."

"And there was I thinking that you were taking crack or smoking, and you've been here playing bowls!" I laughed.

"Is this a game your mother plays?"

"Yeah, sure. She's a good player. But she could never win on this terrain. We are much tougher players than her." Jenkins said this proudly, as though somehow playing bowls here made him 'hard'. I think he had almost convinced himself of this. But not quite.

"Look, I'm not going to say anything about this, *if* you come back to school now. One more bunking off episode, and I'll be on the phone to your mother. Do you understand?" I said, putting on my sternest face

Jenkins thought about this for a second. And then shook his head.

"I can't do that."

"What?" I shouted. "You are trying to negotiate with me, when I could get the pair of you suspended like that!" I clicked my fingers, and then pointed one at Jenkins. He didn't flinch.

"I can't do that, unless you tell the kids that you caught us smoking. If they ask."

This took me by surprise. Jenkins sensed my confusion.

"We can't tell them we were playing bowls, can we? I mean we'll look like a right pair of plonkers. We've got to have done something hard. Otherwise we'll be a laughing stock."

"I can't lie to them either. It'll look like I've gone completely soft if I tell them I caught you smoking and I didn't report you," I said.

"You don't have to say anything. You just don't tell them if they ask," he said.

I sighed. "OK, it's a deal."

The dynamic bowls duo got their stuff together, and walked with their bikes back to the school with me. It was a glorious afternoon with the sun shining, and the blue lake winking in the distance. Tench didn't say much but Jenkins was very talkative.

"You shouldn't leave you know. I just think you shouldn't leave," he said.

"Why not?"

"Well, what am I going to do about A-Level English?"

"Who says you're going to get the grades to do it?" I interjected.

Jenkins blew out his lips. "I reckon I'll get the grades. Scrape a C. That's all you need in this school."

"But you could do a lot better," I said.

"Not with the teachers I've had," he said.

"Hey, look. If you insult my teaching..." I retorted angrily, but Jenkins interrupted before I could continue.

"You just can't take a joke, can you? You're a bit psycho, aren't you?"

This was the thing about Jenkins. I could never relax with him. He was a very clever boy who knew my weak spots and, even after I had been so nice to him, he still liked to probe them.

We got back to school, and Jenkins and Tench disappeared – wending their way to the bike sheds. In the end, Jenkins got a B for English, but got a D for English Literature – which was a miracle considering he hadn't even read the set texts! Tench got Es in both exams. Jenkins returned to the sixth form to do English Language Studies A-Level, and Tench went to Sixth Form College to do some vocational courses.

LEAVING

When I announced that I was going, I was reminded that children don't think about teachers leaving in professional terms. To the most emotional of them, teachers are like parents. When you tell them that you are going it's like announcing that you are going to die.

Pupils frequently asked me why I had to go. I explained that I had a promotion, but they wouldn't accept this.

"Aren't we good enough for you anymore?" they would inquire. I would try my best to explain that this wasn't the case but they still wouldn't understand. In their eyes a shroud had been drawn over me, and a hooded man in a black cape, carrying a scythe, was leading me away towards the horizon.

Billy Johns, in particular, seemed upset and gave me a thank-you present of a lollipop on the last day of term.

This was a huge act of generosity for him.

"You don't really have to go, do you?" he said as he gazed mournfully at his lollipop.

"I'm afraid I do," I said.

"But why?"

"Because I got a promotion at another school."

He considered this. "You could get one here, couldn't you?"

"Not the type I got."

"So what am I going to do now?" he said. He was quite upset. I realised that, to him, I was a father-figure of sorts. Probably more reliable than his own father who was rarely at home. A least I had been more reliable, until I decided to leave: yet another man who was buggering off. But I had my own life to lead. This felt like the right decision for me. It was a selfish decision, but it felt right.

I sensed at the time that a lot of the staff weren't sorry to see the back of me. I could tell just how disliked I was by my leaving present; a cheap tie. Staff were asked to donate money to leaving presents; I don't think anyone donated much for mine.

Even more ill-feeling was generated on my last day because my sixth form group, who were jointly taught by Morgan and myself, decided to go and complain about Morgan to the Headteacher.

Apparently, he didn't teach them anything in the lessons but preferred to talk about his archaeological expeditions. It looked like I had put the kids up to it – which I hadn't – and the Head wasn't happy. He wished me a very curt good luck as he said goodbye to the departing staff, and joked rather sourly that it was good to get rid of a traitor. This raised a big laugh.

***

I look back at Humbards now as my Golden Age Of Teaching.
I had so much energy then! While there were problems, my
overall feeling for the school remains overwhelmingly positive.
I remember sunlit corridors, the trees in the quad, Yolanda's
hair flying free, eager classes and happy children, eccentric,
grumbling but essentially happy staff, and the summery park
beyond – where I had found Jenkins and Tench playing boules.

Of course, I realise I have a ridiculously idyllic view of the
place, but it's a feeling that has never left me. The school actually became a difficult place to teach after I left. The pupils it
took changed and the classes became unruly – according to
some Ofsted inspectors. The cool Mr Woodham, the best
headmaster I have worked with, was edged out and a lot of the
staff left. I suspect he wasn't that great at playing the bureau-
crats' game. While he was excellent at dealing with staff, and
was very approachable, Woodham was less adept at dealing
with pupil indiscipline. You probably need to be a bastard to
be a good Head, and he just wasn't one.

Billy Johns got some GCSEs. He achieved D grades in the
vital English and Maths. This wasn't bad but he could have got
C grades if he had really tried. Apparently, according to a

156

teacher I met some years later, he still talked about me, about how I had wanted him to get his English and Maths GCSEs. Melissa Cruickshank went on to get her A-Levels and go to Bristol University. I was pleased about this because it was probably a major act of rebellion against her parents. They were determined she would go to Oxbridge, where, I was told, she turned down a place.

And Yolanda – beautiful, gorgeous Yolanda – who was my soul-mate for a couple of years, what of her? We met a couple of times after I left, but then all contact ceased. I was told by some other teachers that she had gone to Sussex. I haven't seen or heard of her in years.

I have met a few of the other teachers, though. The most interesting meeting was with the lovely old hippy Art teacher, Juan, who told me one of the most blackly humorous school anecdotes I have ever heard. In many ways it typifies how I feel about the school. Apparently, a couple of years after I left, there was an old boys' re-union, some sort of anniversary, when some octogenarians were taken around the school by the Headteacher, Mr Woodham. These old boys were ecstatic about seeing their alma mater; one was so happy that he insisted upon sitting in the Headmaster's chair, where he promptly died! This put something of a dampener on the old boys' reunion, but Juan was chuckling away about it.

"There could be far worse ways to die, couldn't there? I think for this old boy he had reached the apogee of life by sitting finally, after so many years, in the Headmaster's chair, and he felt there was nothing else left to be done."

PART TWO

TEACHER ON THE RUN

Ah! Mr Henry Pullum! What a wonderful pedagogue he appeared to be in his crisp, linen suit and sunglasses! I had never come across his like before. He exuded confidence, he radiated enthusiasm, he carved great educational dreams with his expressive hands and elaborate discourse. He ran an efficient department – *and* he was an advisor to the government.

The day before term started, he met me and the other department "team leaders" in a trendy gastro pub and gave us all a pep talk.

"You are my magnificent team!" he exclaimed with a clap of his hands – as he ordered us all a round of mineral water and warm goats' cheese salads. "The Head and I have great plans for you all. Spear-heading it all we have Myfanwy, who is supervising the Key Stage 4 curriculum, the lynch-pin of the operation. Then there is Spencer here, the Key Stage 3 team leader, and lastly, but not least, Francis, who will monitor assessment procedures and the deployment of support teachers within the department. Of course, the key thing to think about is results; we get good results, but I need to address the whole issue of Value-Added now. What do you think of the concept of Value-Added, Francis?"[14]

I had, to be honest, been looking out of the window at this point; there was a gang of well-dressed white youths hanging around on the corner of the High Street. They were jeering and laughing. I blinked. And thought for a bit. I didn't actually know what Pullum was talking about; I wasn't sure what Value-Added was.

"Err..." I mumbled.

Pullum smiled and sipped his mineral water. "You have, of course, read the Departmental Handbook which explains all of this. Myfanwy, could you help us out here?"

Myfanwy, who was a short-haired young woman with

[14] Value-added scores. This is the idea that schools should not only score good results, but should improve a pupil's performance over and above what is expected of them, or "add value". So, for example, if a child scores a Level 4 in their Key Stage 2 English test – the test that all state children take when they are ten or 11 years old – they are expected to attain a Level 5 at Key Stage 3. However, if they scored a Level 6 at Key Stage 3, the school would be judged to have added value. There are numerous ways departments can be measured for the average value that they add to pupils' scores.

backwards teeth and dark eyes, reared up her neck nervously and started to talk. And talk. It was really weird. I didn't understand anything she said. It was all facts and figures; stuff about Band Levels at GCSE, employing modular courses to boost results, and Action-Planning C/D borderline students.

It had been a long summer holiday and I wasn't yet in the mood for teaching. I nodded my head vigorously, though, pretending I knew what was going on, and mercifully I was not questioned about anything else.

After our salads, we all walked up the hill to the school to do some intensive "resource-networking". The school was situated on a picturesque site; there was a pond and fountain situated in the middle of a square, which was awash with exotic plants. Many of the modern classrooms overlooked this part of the school. The other part of the school – comprising a cluster of old fashioned buildings and a few, isolated prefabs – was not so prepossessing. My classroom was one of these prefabs, situated well away from the main English suite – where Pullum and Myfanwy taught.

Pullum took off his sunglasses as he guided me into the room. He showed me where my "resources" cupboard was and said that I should ask if I had any questions or queries.

"We pride ourselves on being a very open department. We're always sharing, sharing, sharing. That's the name of the game here. I hope you get a sense of that with our resource-networking," he said, patting me gently on the back.

We returned to the "Resources room" and all sat down around the table. Myfanwy and Spencer then talked about the schemes of work that everyone was doing during the term, identifying the "raising achievement" componentsthat needed to be stressed by every teacher. Again, I felt a bit lost, and didn't have anything to say when Pullum invited me to question them. Although I had been teaching for nearly five years, I realised that I had never worked in a successful department; my first Head of Department had spent most of his time in a cupboard, and the next one had been more interested in knitting and avoiding split-infinitives than "resource-networking" and "Action-Planning C/D borderline candidates".

I spent most of that evening reading the Departmental Handbook – which I had shamefully neglected to peruse during the holidays.

FIRST TEACHING DAY AT BROKERS

I was very tired because I had spent most of the night worrying that I hadn't prepared my lessons according to departmental specifications. Having operated in environments of neglect, I had always prepared my lessons myself, using the National Curriculum and the relevant syllabi as my guides. But things at Brokers were different. Certain "modules" – month-long lesson plans – had to be taught. Set assessment procedures had to be followed. My work would also be monitored every few weeks or so, and I had to make sure that the support teachers in the department were doing their jobs properly.

Nevertheless I decided that I would surreptitiously continue with my own lesson plans for the first couple of weeks – to buy myself a bit of time – and shift to the department's schedule after that.

I decided I would kick off with my first Year 8 class by explaining my acrostic poem, which had been so successful at my last school. But I could see that something was a little bit awry by the way the kids lined up. They were so noisy that I knew that it was pointless trying to shout at them outside my pre-fab hut; their banter didn't appear as if it was ever going to stop. Added to which, I was a bit paranoid that Pullum would see me struggling with such a young class; I didn't want him to get the wrong impression. So I let them file into the classroom without establishing any order. This was a mistake because there was a massive ruck as a tangle of children rushed for their preferred chairs.

Squabbles began immediately between a few children – mostly a group of white-faced, angelic looking boys who appeared quite small for their age.

"Sir, he took my chair! That was my chair," one kid protested with such a victimised look on his face, I would have felt sorry for him if I hadn't seen him elbow his compatriot in the chest just seconds before.

"Just sit down," I said, trying to keep calm.

"But you don't understand, this big boy here is bullying me. I'm only little. He's big. He's got a hairy chin. Look at it," the cherubic-faced rascal said.

I scrutinised the taller boy, and saw that he did indeed have quite a bit of bum-fluff floating around his chin.

"Sir, do you know I'm named after a famous poet? Keats. My name is John Keats," the bum-fluff boy said.

Chaos was engulfing me as I listened. I realised that I didn't have time to engage in this bizarre conversation. I had to get the lesson started. I started telling everyone to sit down. When they didn't hear, I yelled, "JUST SIT DOWN!"

This achieved the desired response and I was able to hand out my acrostic poem. I realised that getting this lot to read it in pairs would not work so I read the poem to them quickly:

Minds are like gardens: they must be tended;

Reading is sunlight for the plants.

Good manners help everyone.

Independence of mind is vital to success.

Listen like a mouse, watch like a hawk.

Believe in yourself and take pride in your work.

Early planning, fluent writing and careful editing are crucial.

Respect your teacher, your environment, and yourselves.

Try hard and you will enjoy yourself!

As I explained the next task, I saw that John Keats and the cherub, who was called Gabriel Tonks, were turning my poem into paper aeroplanes. As I approached they hastily smoothed out the paper and pretended that nothing had happened.

"I think John Keats did better," the bum-fluff said with a croaky laugh.

"Excuse me, I didn't ask your opinion. I want you to write your own poem now, telling me about yourselves. An acrostic," I said.

"What's an acrostic?" Gabriel asked. This irritated me because I had explained what an acrostic was several times already. I knelt down to Gabriel's level and wrote his name in his book vertically down the page.

"Now, what can we write down for G?"

"But why G?"

"Because it's an acrostic," I said.

"I don't like sausages," Gabriel said.

"But that doesn't begin with a G."

"But it's something about me. I don't like sausages or people with bad breath!" he said, waving a hand in front of his nose, and thus indicating that I suffered from halitosis. John Keats and Gabriel burst out laughing at this. In a quieter class, such a cheeky comment would have been noticed by everyone, but this lot were very noisy, gabbling away at each other at the top of their voices. No one else overheard Gabriel's impudence.

I wandered around the class trying to calm people down, but it didn't have much effect. Most of the pupils had got the hang of the acrostic and were producing some reasonable work; the girls, in particular, seemed very focused and bright. But there were clearly a lot of boys who were not especially clever, and quite badly behaved.

It was very early days and they were scoping me out. My yell to get them to sit down had had an effect; I clearly wasn't a complete softie. But as they left the lesson I felt worried. If they had been like this on the first lesson – most kids are well behaved for the first few lessons, before they reveal their true colours – what were they going to be like in a few months' time?

FATAL ACCIDENT AT CHIAPOOPOO

I waited for Year 9 outside the prefab with my arms folded. I reflected that my last lesson hadn't been too bad; heaven knows I had seen worse in Tower Hamlets.

The sun shone brightly as I watched several knots of children bob and twist into view. They were all dressed relatively smartly in their school uniforms. They looked well fed and affluent, and appeared to be full of energy. Energy for making a noise. A very, very loud noise.

In terms of decibel levels this lot were worse than the last. Again, I realised it would be useless to shout at them outside the prefab; they just wouldn't hear me. I resorted to asking them to do up their ties and get into line. At that moment, another teacher appeared. I hadn't been properly introduced to her as yet, but I knew from my timetable that she was scheduled to "support" me during the lesson. In other words, she was there to assist the pupils who found the work difficult. I glanced down at the timetable and read her name quickly again: Mrs Chiapo. She was a Mediterranean-looking woman, with a benign smile and a Cockney accent. I found the exotic surname a bit confusing because of her very London accent.

I was also being pushed and jostled as I entered the classroom with the kids. I hurried to my desk and called for order. I thought about trying to get the pupils to sit in alphabetical order – I had forgotten to do that with the previous class – but I could see that it would involve a big palaver. No one appeared to be listening. Every kid, as in the last class, was chatting merrily away to the person sitting next to them – almost totally oblivious to the fact that they were about to be taught a lesson.

"Excuse me, you are NOT going to sit in these seats!" I

said. "I am your new English teacher, I don't know your names, and I need you sitting down alphabetically."

There was a roar of annoyance. "But we just sat down!"

"I always get put next to a BOY," said a blond, bespectacled girl.

"I NEVER get to sit next to my boyfriend. I love him. I can't be apart from him!" shouted a large buck-toothed girl who was embracing a small, puny boy with a big grin on his face.

"You're having me on, ain't you mate?" said the only Asian kid in the class. He was a tall, skinny youth with some big, gold rings on his fingers. I knew what that meant.

"No! Now I want Rory Addison to be here," I said. This pupil turned out to be the puny boy, in the oversized uniform, sitting next to the massive girl.

A great wail arose from her. "Awww! Whatcha wanna do that for? He's my baby!" she said.

"You have to move," I said, indicating that Rory should sit at the front of the class. He puckered up his face, "I hope I ain't gotta sit next to any dorks."

But he did get up, disengaging himself from the great big girl. I think he was secretly pleased to be free of her grasping. He was a very young-looking thirteen-year-old with a squeaky voice and baby skin. God knows what those two saw in each other. I called out Belinda Bringhurst to sit next to Rory. She was a swotty girl with glasses, and Rory clearly did not like the loss of street cred that was involved in sitting next to her. He slapped his forehead. "Oh, come on! What did I say about dorks?"

He attempted to get up and return to his former seat but the support teacher intervened, standing between him and his lover, and he remained where he was.

The placements went pretty well after that until I came upon the Asian kid's name: Azizur Rahman. He stood up and bunched his hands into a fist and exclaimed, "You ain't doing that mate. No, you ain't."

His lips were compressed, and he appeared very angry. I decided to leave him where he was, and pretended that I wanted him sitting in the place that he was already in. He grinned broadly at Rory as I moved on to the next person. This was a cue for Rory to start bleating.

"How come Aziz gets to stay there, and I've got to sit next to dorks?"

I noticed that Janice, who was Rory's "girlfriend", had her legs spread open and was sitting slouched in her chair. She was grinning widely at Rory, as her tongue flicked around her lips.

"Look, just leave it, OK?" I said to Rory.

"How can I leave it when she's over there and she wants me?" he said in his scratchy, squeaky voice.

"Can you sit up please!" I shouted at Janice.

"Rory! He's being mean to me! Protect me!" she said with dramatic emphasis.

"Don't you diss my girlfriend," Rory said, standing up and making fists with his hands. Everyone laughed at this because Rory was such a tiny character; he couldn't have harmed a Chihuahua.

I was feeling quite agitated. My morning hadn't been going well. I handed out my poem in a bit of a haze, and introduced myself as Mr Gilbert. I then introduced my support teacher, quickly scanning her name on the timetable:

"And for the rest of the year, Mrs Chiapoopoo will be supporting us!"

What possessed me to say this? I had read her name. I could see it was Mrs Chiapo. It bore no relation to poo poo at all. And yet I had said – idiot, moron, and prat that I was – Mrs Chiapoopoo.

The class fell around laughing. I remember mouths stretched open to their fullest extent, teeth glinting in the light, howls of derision and merriment, screeches and screams of hysteria, hands pummelling the desks, feet stamping on the floor. I reddened. Then shut my eyes tightly. Opened them. Still the roaring continued.

I gazed apologetically at Mrs Chiapo, who seemed slightly amused but also somewhat concerned by my mistake. She said, "It's Mrs Chiapo."

More laughter.

"I'm really, really sorry. I just..."

I wanted to leave the classroom there and then. To leave the classroom, and to come back and start all over again. What a fool! But I couldn't. I was in charge of support teachers, I had TWO responsibility points added onto my salary, I had taught in two comprehensives and yet had never been so foolish.

After the class had calmed down a bit, I ploughed on with reading my poem. Not many of them were listening; they chatted idly to each other as I read my preciously carved words. My mistake had seriously undermined my confidence *and* authority. I didn't have the stomach to discipline the class. I gently asked them – amidst the jabbering chatter – if they would get on with writing their own poem. Not many of them did.

Rory was now sitting back with Janice, and Aziz had snuck his chair up to them. Again, I knew that I should remonstrate with them about this, but I didn't have the mental strength. I was clean out of beans. As Bertie Wooster would say, I'd lost my pep! Aziz was giggling with Janice, who was telling him not to, because Rory would get jealous.

"Do you think I should batter him sir?" Rory asked me. "I'd smash his teeth in. Blood everywhere. Mash him up. He'd look a real minger."

"I'm not sure that's a good idea, Rory," I said.

"If he touched me I'd get his balls and twist them around his mum's throat," Aziz said, quite cheerfully, and grinning brightly at Rory.

"Oh you leave my lickle baby's mum alone!" Janice intervened, slapping Aziz flirtatiously on the wrist. Aziz quietened down at this, and I moved on not knowing what to do with them. Their banter, for all its violent imagery, was quite playful.

To my surprise and relief, I found a couple of girls, Prisca and Violet, busy at work on their own poems. They were giggling with real intensity, but appeared to have written a lot:

Piles and piles of manure are
Ready
In the garden. There's a bad
Smell and a teacher is saying Mrs
Chiapoopoo.
Ah, poor dear.

"Very funny," I said, and moved on again, leaving them to their mirth. I found Mrs Chiapo helping out a Chinese girl, Adeline, in the corner of the room. She had only been in the country for a few years, but she seemed to have quite a good command of English; together she and Mrs Chiapo had written a creditable poem. I praised it and then, thankfully, the bell went for the end of the lesson.

When the pupils had gone, I apologised again to Mrs Chiapo. "Ah, don't worry about it mate," she said. "That's the least of my worries."

"What do you mean?"

"I mean being in this bloody place is suffering enough."

"What's wrong with it?"

"Oh, you'll see," she said darkly.

TELLING MR PULLUM

At lunchtime, I slumped down in my chair at the round table in the "Resource-networking" room. I was exhausted, and I still had afternoon lessons to complete. Mr Henry Pullum was busy with grading some students' papers, but when he finished, he looked up and asked me how my first morning had gone.

"Great, it was good," I said with gritted teeth. I felt I couldn't tell him the truth. "Yeah, it was fine."

"Fantastic! And you're all set with implementing the department's schemes of work?"

"Oh yes."

There was a silence. I felt as if I had to fill it, that Pullum was expecting me to say more. He was smiling at me in a knowing fashion; there was a look in his eyes, telling that he knew something. Maybe he had heard about the Chiapoopoo incident. I decided to tell him about what had happened.

Pullum's eye widened. "Oh my goodness me! What a story! Oh Francis, what a thing to say!"

At that point Myfanwy and Spencer entered the room, and immediately Pullum jumped up and told them the story. Soon, the whole room was full of laughter. I was laughing too. These people could see the funny side of things. They were funny people. But just what were they laughing about? Were they laughing at me or with me?

I couldn't decide, but I met Mrs Chiapo a bit later on, and she said that I shouldn't have told them. Now the whole school would know.

I retreated to the staffroom for my lunch. It seemed a much jollier staffroom than my previous one, except that it was full of smoke. Everyone who was laughing was a smoker. And I didn't smoke. As I opened my packed lunch, I realised that I couldn't stand the smoke, especially while I was eating. I left the nameless faces cackling, and returned to the Resources room, where there was still quite a bit of merriment about Mrs Chiapoopoo.

I ate my sandwiches with a faint smile on my face, and distracted everyone with a question about schemes of work at Key Stage 3. Spencer, a bloke-ish ex-post office worker, with a large mop of brown hair and kind eyes, explained what was involved. He seemed quite an obliging character. Not as intimidating as Pullum. Still I really missed Yolanda. I needed a mate like her right now.

I tried to console myself that my Year 10 tutor group seemed relatively docile. They filed into the pre-fab after lunch, sat down and listened in silence as I called out the register.

"Thank you," I said. "You seem like a great group to me. Let's keep this up."

I had seen from the records that most of the kids in this class were from a relatively affluent background – no one was on free school meals. The whole group was white. Brokers' was a more monocultural school than Humbards – which had been quite diverse.

One girl stuck out from the rest. Doreen, a very rotund girl with so much make-up on that it would have taken a spade to shovel it off. Her rouged cheeks, cherry lips, her double-chins, and bobbed hair made her look like she was a middle-aged Madame.

Doreen grinned at me as I left the classroom after the lesson. "Ya look all right to me," she said. "But, nuffink personal or nuffink, I fink you should be a bit more cheerful."

Her words were compassionate; I think she could see I was suffering. I felt bizarrely bolstered by her exhortations as I faced my afternoon classes.

I had A-Level English followed by bottom set Year 10. Both turned out to be good classes. I had actually prepared in some detail for the A-Level English class, because it was a different course from the one I had taught at Humbards. Pullum's course outline was quite unlike I had ever come across in my previous schools; it was detailed and informative. It was helpful!

I handed out the relevant text books, and discovered, to my relief, that the class was willing to listen in silence to my instructions, and various readings from the book. When they were divided into groups, they all got on avidly with the discussion work. This was much more like it.

Likewise, my bottom set Year 10 English, who only numbered twelve pupils, seemed very winnable. They listened to my poem, and attempted to write their own without any disruptions.

They were not clever – I ended up writing quite a bit for them – but they were willing to try.

When I left the school at 4.30pm, having prepared for the next day's lessons, I reflected that things hadn't been that bad. Sure, Year 8 and 9 had been tough, but the other two classes seemed brilliant; the A-Level English were very sparky, full of comments and life, and the Year 10 class needed intensive assistance, but were worth it.

SIX MONTHS LATER – FEBRUARY

MR BEAN TRIES TO TEACH

My eyes opened. It was still dark outside. I looked at the clock on my bedside table. It was three in the morning. The worst time of the night.

I had been waking up at this time regularly for quite a while now. I would listen to the police sirens screaming in the distance, and gaze through the frosty window at the street-lit scene outside, thinking about the day ahead. Thinking, worrying, ruminating. Biting the worst chunks of it off in my mind, and chewing over the same anxieties again and again.

My anxieties could be boiled down to a couple of innocent-sounding numbers and letters: 8X and 9Y. Why oh why had I landed up with 9Y? Children's chuckling faces arose before me in the darkness, their eyes alight with glee as they ran about the room, pulling at each other's shirts, kicking at the tables and the walls.

And then, just as soon as I thought that I'd expunged those demoniacal visions, other devilish faces bubbled up in my mind; this time they were disguised as angels. Innocent, tiny little boys who were constantly making farting noises, flicking stones from elastic bands, placing staples, pins and razor blades on the teacher's chair.

These hellish portraits, all too close to reality, were then replaced by the question I had been asking myself for some months now: why had I left Humbards? What had possessed me to leave that haven for a few extra pounds? The extra money counted for nothing now. I definitely didn't have much enhanced status; I had been viewed as a bit of a hard man at Humbards, but at the Brokers' Academy I suspected I was seen as something of a joke. The Mrs Chiapoopoo incident had ensured that I was perceived more as Mr Bean than a respected teacher.

I found the only thing that comforted me was an audio tape that I had of Jeeves and Wooster. I would turn over the tape and listen to Bertie Wooster fulminate about his horrific aunts, and the latest appalling fiancée he had to extricate himself from. Fortunately, he had his man-servant – his gentleman's gentleman, Jeeves – to sort out all of his problems. And I suspected this was just what I needed; a friendly master-brain who could get me out of this mess.

"Why don't you tell Pullum?" said my wife at breakfast, after I had complained of another sleepless night.

"But you don't understand. I can't tell him. He's a great teacher. Everyone in the department is a really good teacher. Even the probationary teacher is a good teacher. No one has any problems. No one speaks about any problems. I can't tell

Pullum; I'd look incompetent," I said, mouthing a familiar mantra.

"Look, you can't go on like this. You'll be dead before you're thirty at this rate," she said. "You MUST tell him. Get some help!"

I thought about her advice as I travelled south on the train that morning – mercifully against the main commuter traffic. I shook my head. I couldn't tell Pullum; I'd ride this one out. After all, I'd survived Tower Hamlets, hadn't I? I'd do this job for a year, and then if it wasn't better next year, I'd go. I was determined I would stick at it at least for a year with my dignity intact. I wasn't going to let Pullum know.

I put on my best chipper smile as I entered the school that cold, February morning. I didn't need Jeeves. I could be cheerful, and survive this. Only a few months ago, I had been an educational super-creep *par excellence*; I felt certain I hadn't entirely lost my veneer of competence, despite the Chiapoopoo charade. Perhaps some people had even forgotten about it.

I approached the Resources room with a bounce in my step, but it quickly slowed into a cautious trudge when I heard Myfanwy talking to Spencer.

"Why is Francis never around when you need him? He's always slinking off somewhere when I need to speak to him!" she said bitterly.

I cringed. Her complaint had a grain of truth in it. I was finding it increasingly difficult to enter the hallowed precincts of the Resources room. It made me feel ashamed. Teachers always appeared to be studying schemes of work with diligence and enthusiasm there; the intricacies of the latest GCSE syllabus were discussed with passion and knowledge, plans for extra marking and planning sessions at the weekends were hatched over coffee and fat-free biscuits.

I knew I should have been involved in it all, but I was beginning to feel allergic to the thought of doing any extra work outside school. I had tried taking marking home, but it had never got done, and so I had determined to complete all my planning and marking in school, even if it meant staying late. I tried my best to completely and utterly forget about it over the weekends. I never quite succeeded, but I felt that I might die if I didn't do this.

I slunk back to the staffroom, stinging from Myfanwy's opprobrium. I inhaled the cigarette smoke and watched the science, CDT and maths departments cackle over some bawdy joke that one of them was recounting. They always seemed to be having fun. Maybe I should start smoking? Maybe I should start finding obscene jokes about people called Dick and Fanny funny.

I pulled out my register and perused it at a distance from all of them. And then I went to look at the cover sheet. Shit. I was required to cover a Year 9 class on my one free lesson.[15] I stood staring at the notice board, and kept staring. I just wished with all my heart that I didn't have that cover. Why was the wretched teacher away? And then I saw who it was: Cedric Philpot. He'd been away for a year. Permanently off sick.

I'd heard Myfanwy cursing Cedric in the Resources room, "Useless man, he was one of the worst teachers I'd ever seen. Terrible. Couldn't teach for toffee. And then he has the nerve to try and sue the school just because he can't teach."

Even though I had been at the school for six months by then, I'd never seen Philpot. I had only heard that he had walked out of the school one day screaming at the top of his voice that someone had stolen his board rubber.

"I mean, what kind of guy starts screaming about losing their board rubber?" Myfanwy had joked.

After the hysteria about the board rubber, Philpot hadn't appeared in school again. But the Headteacher had received a letter from his lawyer saying that he was off with stress due to the chronic indiscipline of the pupils, and that he was seeking compensation before he resigned his post. All sorts of

---

[15] The Cover Sheet. Often the most informative document in a school. It tells you who is off sick or on a training course. Usually, the senior management are on some training course or other, and a few lowly mainscale teachers are off sick. Long-term sickness can be a dead giveaway that the school is difficult to work in. In some schools, the cover sheets run to numerous pages because there are so many staff off sick. They can't hack it anymore.

complications arose as a result of this, and the school was forced to pay Philpot his full salary, and another teacher to cover his classes, while backroom negotiations went on.

"This school gets good results, the pupils aren't running wild – except in the real duffers' lessons," Myfanwy said.

Her words echoed in my head as I continued staring at the cover sheet. Was I a duffer like Philpot? Would I end up like him – running from the building screaming about my board rubber? No. Of course not. I swallowed hard and clenched my fists. I was not a duffer.

The thought did occur to me that I could cross my name off the cover list and write Myfanwy's instead. No one was watching. The smokers were enjoying another joke; I could see that Spencer had joined them. He was a canny character, one of Pullum and Myfanwy's favourites, and yet he was a bit of a lad too, joining in with the banter. And he was a good teacher – I had this on the seminal authority of Pullum himself. *And* he was a nice bloke. Why couldn't I be a bit more like him?

The noise of the bell made my spine shiver: there was no time now to get to that list. The smokers were rising out of their seats. It was time to move on to register my tutor group.

This lot had definitely got worse in the last few months. They no longer listened to the register in silence and continued chatting as I read out any notices. To begin with, I had shouted for silence and threatened detentions but I'd soon given up. They weren't killing each other. No other tutor group seemed to listen to any of their tutors. I was fighting against a general culture of chat, and it was a pointless, useless fight.[16] At Humbards, there had been a general culture of respect. Silence while a teacher talked was the norm, not the exception. Here, no teacher seemed to expect to be listened to during registration. What was the point in trying to buck the trend for the sake of a mere tutor group? I was basically only expected to register them and hand out school letters.

However, two characters did listen to me: Doreen and her mate Fizzy, who was actually called Felicity. They would sit at the front of the class applying make-up to their already very made-up faces, and would gaze into their mirrors in silence as I called out the register. Doreen was particularly solicitous of me. On a few occasions, she would lean towards me, her double-chins wobbling under the weight of her make-up. "Do ya know you could be quite cute if ya wasn't a teach? I mean, whatcha do it for? Everyone gives ya grief and so many of them kids stink!"

She spoke about the other children as if she wasn't one. I

---

[16] The war against chat: this is a battle that teachers wage year after year, week after week, minute after minute. The human animal wants to make noise and nothing seems to stop it. It babbles, it howls, it blabs, it guffaws, it whispers, it titters. Even in good schools, teachers are rarely listened to on a collective basis. Silence is only achieved with sleep or death – not options open to teachers these days.

think she believed she had been sent to school by mistake; that she was a mature, notable celebrity who had accidentally happened to stray into school for the day. She took an aesorol can of deodorant from her glitzy, tacky, silver-spangled bag and held it up before me. "Here, sir, do you want to take this so that you don't smell no poo-poo?"

She and Fizzy giggled. Word had swept around about the Mrs Chiapoopoo incident in my Year 9 class. And then swept around again. And then again. Six months later, it was still in the school's collective unconscious, bubbling up every now and then in conversations, prompting great guffaws of laughter, and sly giggles. With those two words, I felt I had fatally undermined my authority as a serious teacher forever.

But interestingly Doreen's comments had more to do with sympathy for my plight than mockery of it. She had said to me a few weeks previously that she felt I had said Mrs Chiapoopoo because my classroom stank of poo-poo. And as a result, it was the most natural thing in the world to mispronounce Mrs Chiapo's name like this.

She nudged the deodorant towards me. "Go on sir, just use it, and spray it around. I mean, if a kid gets on yer tits, just whack a bit of this in their face. Well, pretend you ain't done it deliberately or nuffink, but yer could kinda accidentally just go whoosh!" She started spraying the deodorant into the air, and I had to stop her with a friendly shake of the

184

head. She put it away and winked.

As the bell went, and she tottered out of the room with Fizzy, Doreen winked at me again. "Just remember, if any of them moo moos are driving yer loo loo with their poo poos, I'm the chick you wanna see, *comprendez*?" She tapped her finger against her nose, and leered a little lasciviously at me.

I reflected, somewhat mournfully, as I watched the class disappear, that Doreen was just about the only person in the school who was remotely understanding of my difficulties. She knew I was enduring hell. She was right; I would have loved to employ the deodorant weapon, and my classes did stink! Well, it wasn't so much them, it was just this bloody pre-fab, with its squashed walls and airless windows. It seemed to trap the malevolent odours and push them all together, so that it felt like the atmosphere was dripping with grease, sweat, grime, shit and urine. I shook my head. My disgust was running away with me and my Year 8 class were running into me.

Having started as a rumble in the distance, they now came tumbling into the pre-fab, making the walls shake and the floor quake.

I just watched them, with my arms folded, as they pushed and shoved each other in order to reach the best seats. Perhaps the surest indication that I had lost it with this class, was that the naughtiest kids always wanted to sit at the front, next to the teacher's desk; it was the best vantage point from which to plant sharp objects on the teacher's chair.

Today Gabriel Tonks and John Keats were so concerned to get to the front that they grabbed the seat right next to the teacher's table. This resulted in a tussle. They both shouted to me at the top of their voices that it was their place.

"Sir, he's bullying me! He's feeling my bum," Gabriel screeched. "He's a paedo! Sir, do something! I'm dying!"

John Keats' throatier voice intervened with: "I have to sit here. It's my eyes. I can't see the board otherwise."

There were a few other fights going on in the far corners of the room that seemed a bit more serious, and I moved onto them – I knew from bitter experience that Gabriel never listened to me, and that, short of physically manhandling one of them, neither would sit in the seat I wanted them to.

Two other little boys were busy pushing their table into the backs of some girls, shouting at them that they were "mingers". I was surprised because I had never seen this lot tussling before. I stopped to ask them why they were so angry. The story emerged in dribs and drabs that Sophie, Hilary, Gordon and Peter had all gone to the school disco. They had fallen out because the girls had drunk all the boys' Irn-Bru.

"I leant her my can. I was just being friendly, and she drunk it all," Peter said, pointing an accusing finger.

Sophie turned around and pouted. "I only had a sip. You said I could have a sip."

"But not drink the whole can."

"She didn't drink the whole can," Hilary shouted. "She only had a sip!"

I couldn't believe I was hearing this. Panic was beginning to rise in me. If the good kids were beginning to fight each other, then what was going to happen to this class?

I exploded. "This is pathetic! I have a whole scheme of work to teach and you are arguing over a sip of Irn-Bru! Just sit down, get your books out and do the work!"

The disco group were taken aback by my fury. But the rest of the class were noisy enough not to notice. I now ran to the front because I saw that Gabriel and John Keats were rolling about underneath the table. I felt like yanking them apart, but I knew I'd be in court if I did, so I bent down my head and asked them to sit in their seats. Shouting at them was pointless.

They did as they were told, and with good humour, pretending that they hadn't been play-fighting at all. "I was just tidying up," Gabriel said, putting on his most angelic face. "I was picking litter off the floor."

This was typical of Gabriel. He was perhaps the naughtiest little boy I had ever come across; constantly fighting, cussing and never doing any work. But he had an image of himself as a very well-behaved boy. When I remonstrated with him for doing something ghastly, he would often reply that he was carrying out an entirely harmless activity; if caught twisting a kid's wrist, he would say he was checking the time, if stopped from pushing someone from their chair, he was preventing the furniture from being vandalized; if writing on the board, he was doing a presentation. On the couple of occasions, when I had seen him fiddling around near my desk, he had surely said that he was checking to see if my seat was "safe" to sit on. This was a moot point, because I was finding with increasing regularity that my seat had drawing-pins and staples on it. I was never actually able to catch Gabriel doing it, but I knew it was him.

I dished out the text books that I kept in the cupboard by my desk. I was now following Henry Pullum's schemes of work; they weren't bad at all. At Humbards, where I'd had well behaved classes, I would have had a great time, but here the tasks were not conducive to order as they involved a lot of group work.[17]

Today we were studying a translation of *Beowulf* by Kevin Crossley-Holland. It was a lovely book, beautifully illustrated and marvellously well-written – perhaps a little too well

---

[17] Group work. Many educational studies seem to show that group work is tremendously useful for students in that it helps them become independent learners, improves pupils' ability to co-operate and negotiate and fosters beneficial argumentative thought. Unfortunately, the pupils who need to do it the most are usually the ones who are utterly incapable of doing it without fighting or going right off task. It's an excuse for a ruck. Unless a school makes a really unified effort to instil such values into pupils, group work will always fail. Cf Rhys Griffith's wonderful *National Curriculum, National Disaster* for more information.

written for Gabriel Tonks and some of his compatriots. The descriptions of the monster Grendel, who emerges from the foggy swamps of England in order to grab and eat various innocent Anglo-Saxon warriors, were lost on them – although the violence did provide a frisson of interest. The group of five that included John Keats and Gabriel Tonks struggled to read the material because Gabriel kept interrupting them by a) kicking them under the table b) trying to pinch one of them c) throwing the book on the floor d) getting out of his seat and running around the room.

Only two of the groups were actually doing what they were supposed to be doing: sharing the reading of the book around the group, and discussing the questions on the worksheet. The other groups were either not reading anything and having a chat, or not reading and getting involved in fights. Not wanting to interrupt the two groups that were working, I tried to move Gabriel to one of the chatty but not violent groups. The net result of this was a game of musical chairs. Gabriel would sit in his allotted seat for a few minutes and then go back to the former group, pushing the person who had replaced him out of the way. When he saw me coming he would then go back to the group I had moved him to, once again pushing aside the hapless soul who had gone back to his original seat.

Perhaps because Gabriel was such a tiny boy, no one minded being shoved around by him; no one actually hit him back. But they did remonstrate, complaining bitterly that he was always whacking them. Occasionally, a pupil would put his head in an armlock but not for very long because when they did, Gabriel would emit a high-pitched squeal which was deafening and extremely unpleasant; it sounded like a pig being strangled.

"Sir, I'm reading! I'm reading!" he said enthusiastically as I approached. "Look, I'm here."

"You're not reading. I've just seen you run up and down the classroom for the last five minutes," I said in a resigned voice.

"I wasn't. That was someone else. I never. I never. I'm reading," he said, looking at me with his doe eyes.

I turned around in disgust.

It wasn't worth the argument. Gabriel lived in his own parallel world where he always did the work, where he was a good and clever reader, and where he was constantly well-behaved. Nothing I ever said seemed to disabuse him of this notion. This boy was so asinine that he just wasn't worth the effort. But as I was walking away he shouted out again, this time at the top of his voice: "I am reading sir! I've got a book! I brought it to school all by myself!"

I glanced over my shoulder, and saw, to my amazement, that he did have his own reading book. However, when I scrutinized it more closely I saw that it had a bright yellow cover, and a gaudy picture on it. Oh God, it wasn't! It couldn't be!

How could the boy have the nerve?

He was holding a Noddy book by Enid Blyton! And he was now reading it at the top of his voice. Badly. With a big, shameless grin on his face. John Keats was killing himself with laughter. He looked like he might vomit.

"And Big Ears said to the Golliwogs," Gabriel pronounced slowly with a huge grin on his face. He was almost proud that he could say the words.

I raised my hands to my face and cringed. I felt like crying and laughing at the same time. This boy, who was not a deprived boy, or mentally impaired, who had been taught in supposedly good schools for eight years, COULD SCARCELY READ NODDY! And he was laughing about it! What had he been doing all of this time? I thought of all the money that had been wasted on the little imp! Thousands and thousands of pounds of taxpayers' money down the drain!

Eventually, conscious that too many people were now listening to his laboured reading, Gabriel stopped.

"I'm really good at reading, ain't I sir?"

"Well done, Gabriel, I'm really proud of you. Now I want you to finish that book by the end of the week, and I'll give you a merit for it," I said, doing my best not to reveal my twisted smile of pain and embarrassment. "Let's get this reading thing moving!"

John Keats wasn't having any of this. "You can't do that.

You can't give him a merit for reading Noddy! It's Noddy sir! He's reading Noddy! That's not proper writing. It's got Big Ears and Mr Plod and Golliwogs in it! That's not reading."

"It's words on the page. He was reading them. Which is more than he's done for the last five or six years in school, I bet."

John Keats considered this for a moment. "You're right there. I was with him in primary school, and he…" Both kids broke into more peals of laughter at this point.

"He made one teacher leave, and there was this other teacher who used to lock herself in the cupboard when he went near her."

"Shut up you!" Gabriel said with a disguised smile. He was obviously proud of this achievement. "She used to let me play with the clay. She wouldn't have done that if she didn't think I was a good boy. Only good boys get to play with the clay, she would say."

"That's b-s! She only let you play with that clay 'cos it was the only thing that shut you up. You were the worstest I ever saw."

"Worse than with me?" I asked, now genuinely interested.[18]

---

[18] Learning about other teachers' failings from the kids. This is something that teachers should not indulge in but I fear it happens rather a lot. Kids are often coaxed by teachers to talk about how badly behaved they are in other lessons, compared with the one they are currently in. It is one of the few times when teachers can feel good about themselves: knowing that these children are worse in other lessons.

"Oh, he's good for you sir. You should see what he's like in the other lessons. He's got this screwdriver and he unscrews all the tables and chairs. No one knows it's him, but that's what he does. And he scratches everything with it. Sometimes he stabs you with it."

"Shut up! Shut up you ucky mucky ucky uck-bag!"

This was a veiled form of swearing that had swept through the school recently; leaving the "f" off "fuck".

"Gabriel, language please!"

"I wasn't swearing!"

I realised that I was about to get drawn into another of Gabriel Tonks's vortex of claim and counter-claim – one of his specialities – and I decided to duck out of it. By walking off right now. I would hear about the poor primary school teacher in the cupboard some other time.

Meanwhile, I had to consider what to do since nearly three quarters of the class were not reading. I thought about asking them to read the book silently or to follow me reading it. Both options were tricky. They involved getting the class to shut up. Still, how else were we going to read the flaming text? Pullum was wanting to observe me teaching some of the department's specially devised lessons in a couple of weeks.

I decided to shout at the top of voice that I wanted quiet. No one listened. I repeated my request, walking around the class. I did this for about five minutes, and, at the end of it, most of the class were listening. I said that I was now going to read the text with the whole class listening. Immediately, several hands shot up.

"Sir, sir, I want to read! Let me read!"

It was Gabriel. And John Keats. Since I had nearly lost my voice trying to get quiet, I decided to give my vocal chords a rest and let them read.

It was agonising. They laboured over Crossley-Holland's sentences painfully, and soon the class was chatting again. I had lost my energy by this time to shout again for quiet. I wrote an exercise on the board; they had to write a modern-day version of the story, imagining that Grendel came to eat children from Brokers' Academy. My own fantasies began to take over as I wrote this down: I saw the slavering, blood-stained lips and limbs of Grendel stomping into the school. His hands smashed through the windows of the pre-fab and grabbed a handful of children, munched them for a bit, and then spat them out into the school pond. His great feet obliterated the desks and tables and annihilated the Resources room, sending the school statistics sailing into the blue air. The screams of Myfanwy filled the air as all of her precious books disappeared down Grendel's gullet. Everywhere people were fleeing the school never to return again.

My eyes snapped back to reality.

I was amazed. My exercise had worked as I had been

day-dreaming. Everyone had been busy planning out what might happen. Even Gabriel and John Keats were interested.

"But what happens in the story?" he asked.

I gave him a précis of *Beowulf*, and his eyes widened.

"So I could make Grendel a teacher in disguise who has this monster in his belly and it splats out of his stomach and all his guts are on the floor, and he is screaming, and he dies, and then the monster comes and bites everyone's brains out?"

"I suppose so," I said dubiously. "Although that isn't what happens in *Beowulf*. Beowulf kills Grendel, and then Grendel's mother tries to get her revenge. She is much more terrifying than Grendel."

"What if the mother comes down in a spaceship?"

"You could do that," I said, hastily moving on.

By the end of the lesson, I felt quite pleased with myself because most of the class were writing their stories; writing the story seemed to have given them the incentive to actually finish reading the short book on their own. As the bell went for break I chalked up a minor victory for myself.

FEAR AND LOATHING WITH YEAR 9

Over the last five months, my real enemy-number-one had become the 13-year-old Azizur Ahmed, one of the few Bengali pupils in the school. He was admittedly the bad boy of the school; he'd been suspended for smoking and fighting; he'd been arrested for joy riding; and his brother was about to go to prison for attempted murder. I'd never come across someone who was so full of hatred; the children I had taught in Tower Hamlets were pussy-cats compared with him. Azizur hated teachers, hated school, and had me down as someone he could be especially belligerent to.

On this bleak, raw February morning, things began badly. The first thing I saw, when I returned after my extra-strength instant coffee in the staffroom, was Azizur pushing over Rory Addison. Azizur, who was normally very friendly with Rory, said, "What did you do that for? Why are you picking on me?" I could tell from his manner that this was no joke.

Rory bleated that he hadn't done anything. He seemed quite frightened.

I strode over, incensed by this unprovoked attack and told Azizur that he should leave the classroom immediately. He'd only been in my lesson five minutes. Azizur then turned on me and said, "Why are you picking on me? I ain't done nuffink. His arse got in the way of a chair. What's wrong with your eyes?"

I repeated that I wanted him to leave the classroom. This was a cue for Rory to pipe up and say that Azizur hadn't really done anything; he'd just tripped over. "Don't pick on him sir, he ain't done nuffink," Rory said.

I saw a little conspiratorial smirk spread over Rory's lips as I turned to face Azizur. "Yeah, just listen to him. You ain't right," Azizur said, laughing loudly.

Azizur was standing up, his hands bunched up into fists. His posture and absolute refusal to listen to my demands scared me. At Humbards, I would have filled out a slip and told Azizur to go and see a senior teacher in the dining room. If he had refused to go I would have gone and fetched the senior teacher myself. But there was no such system at Brokers. In fact, sending children out of the class was very much frowned upon.

I decided to let this one ride, told Azizur and Rory to get on with their work and prayed that they wouldn't do anything more. This was an error. If you make a demand like the one I had made, you have to carry it out or otherwise your authority is eroded.

Azizur started laughing.

"Ain't you going to send me out, then?" he jeered.

This took me by surprise. I thought about it for a minute.

"All right then, perhaps you'd better go out," I said.

Azizur laughed again. "You can't send me out. I didn't do anything. Like Rory said, it was an accident," he sneered.

This was torture. I felt like a mountain climber scaling a sheer cliff face without any grappling hooks. I just couldn't find any purchase with Azizur, or in fact with any of these kids.

They just never, ever conceded an inch.

"You'd better go," I said.

This caused an explosion of indignation.

"But that's so unfair. I ain't done nuffink!"

I made the mistake of trying to square up to Azizur, of trying to dominate him with my superior physical bulk. I stood over him and tapped the back of his chair. I felt like yanking him out of it.

"Get out now! Just get out of here!" I shouted.

Azizur snarled, "Oh you stupid tosser!" and lurched out of his seat, kicking the table in the process. He narrowly avoided barging into me. Once outside the classroom though, he caused more problems by yanking the door open and slamming it shut. Next, he pressed his face against the glass and hammered against the hardboard walls of the pre-fab.

Somehow I staggered through to the end of the lesson, but my ship was bobbing about in violent seas and had sprung several serious leaks.

GETTING HELP

I had spent the best part of five months assiduously avoiding seeking any help from Pullum. After all, I had sold myself to Pullum and the Head at the interview as a super-competent teacher, who could more than handle the classes in a respectable suburban comprehensive. Besides, I looked at the other teachers in the department and believed that they weren't having any of the problems I was. Teachers who were far more junior than I was, and without any rank, seemed to be getting along just fine.

Or so I thought. No one really talked about the behaviour of the children in the staffroom in the way they had done at Humbards. At my previous school it had been a constant moan; teachers vented their frustrations about the difficulties they were having, and confessed to their friends the truth about what was going on in their classrooms without feeling ashamed. No one did that at Brokers. Virtually the only talk that went on in the Resources room was about curriculum planning, or complaining about Cedric Philpot. It was all very professional.

That lunch-time, when there was no one else around, I approached Pullum in the most professional manner possible, and explained that I had a problem with Azizur Ahmed. Pullum looked around to check that no one was listening, and then suggested that we went to an empty classroom where we would not be heard. Once we were safely out of earshot from everyone, he took out his notebook and scribbled a few notes.

I gulped. This was my big moment. My confession to the High Priest of Education. I trembled a little. All the fear and resentment that I felt about my teaching was just waiting to surge out of my mouth like an unstoppable geyser.

I swallowed hard. I was feeling nauseous. It felt as if my words might come out as vomit.

Pullum was tapping his pen, waiting for me to talk. I had to say something. Eventually, I blurted: "They're just not listening to anything I'm saying. They're not doing the work. I don't know what to do. I've tried giving them detentions, I've tried changing the work."

Pullum frowned. I was unnerved by the severity of his tone when he said, "You know Francis, you shouldn't be telling me these things. You were taken on because you are an experienced teacher who should be able to handle this type of classes. You have an important position of responsibility in the department, and you're hardly setting an example to the more junior members of the department if your classes are behaving like this."

I didn't know how to reply to this. Instinctively, I felt that he was right. I should be ashamed of myself for being so incompetent. I should have a grip on these classes and I shouldn't be whingeing away to my Head of Department. If I had a problem I should be able to fix it myself.

"Of course you're right, I'll sort this out myself," I said. "Thanks for listening to me. I mean, it's not like it's all bad. My sixth form class are good, my bottom set Year 10s are well behaved, and my Year 7s. It's just these Year 8s and 9s."

Pullum let out a sigh of relief. I had said something positive. "See, things are not that bad," he said. "You just need to follow school policies through with your other classes, and everything will be well. Try to relax a little. You seem very tense."

"But what is the school policy for badly behaved children? Maybe there should be a code of conduct? You know, a set of rules that the children should follow."

"I don't think that is necessary," he said. "It's really up to the individual teacher to sort out their own problems. You can't have management always nannying the teachers."

"But the trouble is that none of the kids are aware about what is acceptable or not. And there is no set guidance about giving detentions. It leaves everyone floundering a bit."

"I think you'll find most of the teachers are very happy here. And prigs are never welcomed in any school. But you're not one of those are you Francis?" said Pullum, snapping his notebook shut.

"No. No. Of course not... maybe I should phone the parents of these children. See if that has any effect," I suggested hastily, not wanting to seem completely without ideas.

Pullum tapped his notebook against the table and stood up, glancing at his watch. "Yes, yes, I would try that."

I stood up as well. He didn't look at me. I felt ashamed; I was a a hopeless moaner in his eyes, I was sure of it.

"Thanks for helping me out," I offered, desperate for some kind of approbation.

Pullum smiled. "It's my pleasure. And anytime you've got any sort of problem you know who you can come to," he said.[19]

DEAD TEACHER WALKING

That night, armed with their phone numbers, I called the parents of Gabriel Tonks and John Keats. I had not met them at a parents' evening yet: that happened at the end of the year. Mrs Tonks's voice sounded sweet, mellifluous and full of concern at the end of the line. I explained what had been going on in my classroom: the inability to do any work, the constant fighting, cussing and cheek. She listened patiently and said, "Oh dear oh dear, you poor thing. What has he been putting you through? Are you tearing your hair out?"

"Maybe," I said.

---

[19] <u>Blaming the teacher.</u> This is a favourite occupation of the government, some parents and senior management in many schools. Teachers are an easy target. Obviously though, there are a multitude of factors when considering why pupils misbehave in school: social and psychological background being the chief among these. The school does have a major role to play but as a collective institution. It is ridiculous to expect one teacher to solve pupils' problems if there isn't a co-operative culture in the school. It is only when the pupils get the feeling that teachers are fully supported by the school that they start to behave properly because they know there will be real consequences if they are disruptive.

"The trouble is, you see, he's also like that at home. He's really a lovely, little angel at heart. No more than a baby really. He's very young for his year, you know. And did ever so well with his painting at primary school. He used to make me lovely pictures and come home and tell me that they were specially for me. But I think he's fallen in with a bad lot at school. This John Keats. Not a good influence. Thinks he has to imitate the big boys, when he's no more than a baby really. He babies around like that at home. Always rushing around throwing things, and coming out with some dreadful language," she said in a rushed, whispered voice. I got the sense that she was frightened that Gabriel might hear her.

I also realised that this was a useless exercise; it was like asking a piece of dead meat to get rid of the vultures. She was dead meat. I was dead meat. We were Gabriel's sport, his sustenance; humiliating us was how he got his kicks.

Mrs Keats was remarkably similar in her response; full of concern, eager to help, but utterly and totally without any authority to impose any discipline upon her son. He was probably far worse with her than he was with me. I could hear him screaming in the background as I spoke to her. What had happened to the parents in this country? It appeared in their anxiety to please their children, they had lost control over them. These were not poverty-stricken, single mothers living in council flats that I was talking to; these were happily married, financially secure women whose children were running riot.

These phone calls both reassured and unnerved me. Reassured because it was obvious that I was not the only one who was the victim of these kids' cheek, and unnerved because they offered no solution except to plough on, remain patient, and hope that things would improve. I couldn't help feeling that I was a "Dead Teacher Walking" – a teacher under a sentence of death, just waiting for the day of execution. Weirdly enough, my acceptance of the ghastliness of the situation, made me a bit calmer, and a little less anxious, but only a little.

FIVE MONTHS LATER – MAY

I am standing in the classroom when suddenly I realise I am naked. I have nothing to cover my modesty except for the worksheets I have piled up on the desk beside me. Luckily, there are no kids around. I still have time. Snatching some Pritt-Stick from my bag, I desperately start plastering the worksheets with glue, and pasting them onto my bare flesh.

By the time, my Year 9 arrive I am ready; I have clothed myself from head to toe in paper. Even my face is concealed in grammar exercises. I have left a narrow slit for my mouth, nose and eyes. I can see and I can speak, but otherwise I am entirely armoured with resources. However, I haven't thought about the children. They enter the classroom brandishing Hoovers. Giggling hysterically, they switch on the machines and I find all my worksheets, which I had so assiduously stuck onto my body, being yanked off by the suction. I try to stop the worksheet clothes from coming off but it is useless. I tumble through the air with the paper and hurtle down the pipe of a vacuum cleaner.

I woke up and found my wife sitting up beside me in the bed. She was tugging my arm. "What is it? What is it?"

My brain was still foggy from the dream. The darkness of the bedroom felt like inside walls of the vacuum cleaner's pipe. Dusty, claustrophobic, suffocating. My skin was slicked with sweat.

"You were screaming," Erica said. "You were screaming at the top of your voice. It was scary. It woke me up."

I told her my dream. She listened, "Don't you think it's time you just gave it up? I mean, there are other things you could do."

These words soothed me. Yes, I wasn't completely washed up. I could find something else. I could sign on at a temp agency in the city and find work. I could go back to university and get yet another qualification. I could do anything. Anything but teach!

I had become quite friendly with my cleaner at Brokers', Madge, because I had had to apologise to her so many times for the shocking state that the room got into: graffiti on the desks, litter on the floor, scribble on the walls, spray-can glitter and confetti on the board, great chunks taken out of the door and so on. "You poor sod," she said once. "You have to teach these animals." She always looked at me with real feelings of pity.

I had stopped going into the Resources room entirely now, and only went into the staffroom at lunch-time where I assiduously read the *Guardian*, not speaking to anyone. I liked the beginning of the day because Doreen and Fizzy would always arrive early to tell me about their outrageous exploits the night before. Today, as they normally did, they arrived plonking their glitzy handbags on the table in front of me and produced all sorts of make-up boxes. They chatted as they angled mirrors at their faces and covered themselves in pancake. Doreen was going to change her name to Dee because some guy at Flakeys, the local night club, had said that that suited her better. He'd bought her some vodka jellies and said he worked in garage. Doreen smiled a wonky smile, "I was well pissed sir! I mean them jellies they do the works!"

She was about to expand upon this point when Pullum entered the pre-fab. This was a real shock because he never, ever came into the classroom unless it was to observe me. He'd seen me with my Year 12 class – a lovely, civilised class – and written a very favourable report about me. We'd never discussed the poor behaviour of my other classes again.

He smiled a trifle nervously. I think Doreen made him queasy. But he smiled anyway, "Francis! I have a treat for you! You're going on a trip this afternoon! I've booked the school van for you to take your Year 12 out on a little trip to the Dulwich Picture Gallery. There's a delightful exhibition on of Romantic Art. I thought it would be useful to put your study of Frankenstein in context."

"Oh great," I said. I had never driven the school van before but I felt that this would be churlish to bring up. Pullum genuinely seemed to want to cheer me up.

"So sign out the van with the PE department. Roger Smith said he would explain everything to you this lunch-time, and, Bob's Your Uncle, one great school trip is yours for the taking? Pretty good, heh?"

He departed with these words. Doreen sneered as she added some more eyeliner to her already encrusted eyelashes, "I don't trust 'im sir. Not being funny or anything but 'e seems stuck up to me."

Fizzy agreed. "Yeah, 'e is. But a good teacher."

"It don't matter whether he is or he ain't. Sneaky is sneaky."

"Er, Doreen, you shouldn't be talking about Mr Pullum like that," I intervened.

Doreen cackled. "Come on sir, yer lurve it really, you can't get enough of it," she winked at me.

I snorted that was rubbish, but I reddened with embarrassment as well.

"Go on just admit it, yer lurve it, yer just lurve it!" Doreen persisted, sensing my discomfort. I got up from my desk and walked over to another group of children. As I walked around the class, I realised that everyone was friendly enough towards me. Ever since, I had stopped threatening detentions and just accepted the noise levels at registration, the animosity that some pupils had felt towards me had vanished.

So why was I having nightmares? I shouldn't have been. The pupils in my tutor group, although noisy, were now perfectly amenable. They answered the register, and eagerly offered their homework diaries for me to sign. Having descended into a trough of misbehaviour during the winter, they were on the mend: they were actually quite organised and co-operative.

Likewise, my Year 8 class, while not transformed, were far, far better. They always arrived in their customary high spirits. I had entirely dispensed with the notion of getting them to line up or even to listen to the register. Instead, I wrote the tasks that they had to complete on a worksheet, and gave Gabriel Tonks and John Keats the job of handing out the sheets. These two had thrived in this position of responsibility. They enjoyed informing me of the students who hadn't completed the homework.

The amazing thing was that these children, for all their incessant chatter, liked completing the work as long as it was interesting. I had come across similarly noisy classes in Tower Hamlets and opted for the same technique, a worksheet for everything. However, in that school the problem had been that the majority of the pupils' literacy levels were so low, they couldn't complete even the simplest fill-in-the-gaps sheets. Here, the pupils had reading ages that roughly matched their own ages, and nearly all of them could write fluently, if not accurately. They enjoyed reading instructions by themselves and could read a chapter of a book on their own without teacher intervention. This meant that my exercises could be challenging. We were currently studying a play about a group of students who murder their teacher. The class loved it, and the exercises that Pullum had devised to accompany it: to write an instruction booklet entitled "21 ways to murder your teacher"; write a newspaper article based on the murder; construct a detective story that included the murder; and produce a funeral oration.

The class was a hive of activity. Everyone was on task, either writing their newspaper article or reading the play in pairs. But this didn't mean I could relax. Gabriel Tonks and John Keats made constant demands for me to check their work, to stop their partner from copying off them (as if!), and so on. Their play fights were now reduced to about one or two a lesson:

the ongoing ruck of previous lessons had been significantly reduced as I got to know them better. I had also introduced a discipline book where I wrote down their misbehaviour, detailing what they had done. If they were noted down twice in a lesson, they got a detention. This seemed to work. I no longer bothered shouting at them. I just wrote down what they were doing in the book.

"No, no, I beg you sir. Don't write me down. That terrible book. I hate that book," John Keats pleaded as I whipped out my discipline book having seen him whacking another pupil's chair with his fist. He wanted to take the kid's Gameboy, and his victim was not being co-operative. Keats returned to his chair as I wrote down this information in the book. I said nothing to him, but held up one finger indicating that if one more incident took place he would be in detention.

I had won! In a sense I believed I had beaten the class down. By turning up day after day, by plodding on with the coursework, I ensured that they produced something every lesson now. At the end of the lesson, I would collect their books and mark it thoroughly, praising their efforts wherever I could.

Likewise, I was winning with my Year 9 class since Azizur had been permanently excluded for numerous acts of intimidation. My approach was almost identical to the Year 8 class: to write a worksheet with interesting tasks upon it, and monitor every pupil individually. And they, like the Year 8 class, worked because they were interested in the subject matter. Pullum really was an excellent Curriculum Leader in this regard: he'd written schemes of work that were entertaining and relevant to the National Curriculum.

No mean feat. The unit of work based on Roald Dahl's short stories was an absolute winner. The pupils were fascinated by the stories and liked attempting to write their own ones that contained macabre twists.

Now, I bet you're really beginning to wonder: why *was* I having nightmares? I think it wasn't actually what was happening that was bothering me, it was what could happen. At this point I was preparing lessons and marking work within an inch of my life. It was nerve-wracking, tough, relentless work, and, amidst it all, I felt as if I was losing my appetite for the whole thing. Surely, there must be an easier way of making a living?

ENGLISH CLUB

One of the duties I had been assigned by Pullum was to run an "English club" once a week. This would take place during a lunch-time for pupils who wanted some help with their English homework, or wanted to do some English exercises on their own. Unsurprisingly, no one really wanted to come of their own accord. I had a smattering of keen Year 7 pupils in the first few months of the club but the numbers soon tailed off. Instead, I used the club as cover to put my exasperating Year 8 class in detention.

Technically, I wasn't supposed to do this; Pullum had made it clear that the pupils should be coming to the club of their own free will, that they should view English as something pleasurable not as a punishment. I was inclined to agree with this in theory, but in practice I acted differently – not least because Pullum would get sniffy when he checked the register of the club and saw that only one or two pupils had come along. "You should be enthusing them more than this, Francis! They should be getting excited about English. Can't you try some advertising or do something that they want to do? Maybe put a survey out, and see what might be done."

I was too exhausted and disillusioned to do any of these things. I decided to cheat instead. I put my Year 8s in detention in the club, and put their names on the register. This way I kept up my numbers and kept Pullum off my back.

Surprise, surprise, who was in English club every week? You've guessed it! Gabriel Tonks and John Keats! They were my regulars – they also had detentions after school from me; their behaviour was incorrigible. They were always fighting, or mucking around, or throwing things.

Every now and then, Pullum would pop his head around the door of the computer room – where English club was taking place – and he would smile at Gabriel and John, who he didn't know – he only taught upper school classes – and would say, rubbing his hands together. "You know, you boys really look like you've got a bright future ahead of you! You seem very keen to me."

They would both nod. They liked the image that Pullum had of them as being very keen students – as long as other pupils weren't around to listen. Once, after Pullum left, John turned to me and said, "Does he know we're in detention?"

I didn't reply to this. John Keats chuckled in his inimitable throaty way, "He doesn't, does he, sir? He thinks we want to be here! You told him that, didn't you?"

I harrumphed that Keats could think that if he wanted. But Keats wouldn't let go of his revelation. "You should pay us for coming here. We're making you look good. Come on sir, where's the money?"

Gabriel, who hadn't really realised the implications of Keats's perception, piped up at this: "Yeah sir, you should give us your money. We heard from somewhere you were a millionaire. You owe us money."

"How come you thought I was a millionaire? Do you really think I would be doing this job if I was a millionaire?" I said, suddenly catching my breath at the thought of having such riches.

Gabriel thought about this for a second and then said,

"Would you give up this job if you had the wonga?"

Keats slapped Gabriel on the back and laughed, "Come on you gay boy, he wouldn't go near this school if he had the wonga. You're such a dork!"

I winced. I had been OK about the conversation until now. "It isn't an insult to call someone gay," I said.

"I never said it was," Keats snapped. "You only thought that. I'm glad Gabe is gay."

"I'm not gay, you bum-fluff!"

"You've had more pricks behind you than the Tottenham goal-keeper!"

"You've got, got…" Gabriel was lost for insults and resorted to piling into Keats with his fists, who responded with some enthusiastic jabs to his stomach and back.

It only took a few seconds, but from having a reasonably jokey, if slightly risqué conversation, the two boys now embarked upon quite a vicious fight.

"Shut up, shut up! Just shut up!" I yelled at the top of my voice. I hadn't shouted at these two like this in a while and at my bark they both stopped their fisticuffs. Keats smiled up at me from Gabriel's arm lock.

"You should do that more often you know, sir. Shout a bit more. You don't shout enough."

I waved them towards the computer. This sort of teacher training advice was not useful. "Come on you two, you've got some homework to do. Let's get on with it."

RORY ADDISON'S BIG NIGHT

While I was beginning to adjust to my Year 8s, my Year 9s were different. I didn't seem to have the same authority over them; they never turned up for detentions unless I collected them from a class at the end of school, and besides getting a detention didn't seem to alter their behaviour.

Year 9 were altogether harder – in every respect. In particular, I had begun to demonise Rory Addison in my mind. I had begun to view him as a sort of terrible hobgoblin, a vicious sprite, the like of which you might find in a painting by Goya. But the trouble was Rory was not in a painting, nor was he a phantom. He was very real, and his small, squeaky-voiced, rat-faced antics really got under my skin.[20]

I know I shouldn't have thought about him like this. I know I should have recognized that his overbearing mother and distant, cold father, both of whom I had met at a parents'

---

[20] <u>Demonising pupils.</u> This is one of the worst traps that teachers can fall into. They think a pupil has specifically got it in for them, that everything that pupil does is aimed at spiting them. The truth is, even if a pupil has a definite animosity towards a teacher, there will be other reasons for their hatred that are nothing to do with the teacher. Becoming paranoid about pupils is the first sign that a teacher is cracking up.

evening, were not bringing him up in a suitable fashion. But I just couldn't bring myself to feel any pity for him.

Perhaps because he was such an inadequate, and obviously pre-pubescent specimen, he was constantly looking for ways to prove his manhood to the class. Somehow he had maintained the fiction with the class that he was something of a stud. Janice, the strapping and fully developed girl who had been so devoted to him at the beginning of the year, was still very much attached to him. Now, she was an even bigger, blowsier girl. A predilection of hers was to bury Rory's thin form in between her voluminous breasts.

This was awkward to deal with. Seeing Rory buried in Janice's chest was a comic sight but, while it wasn't massively disruptive, it was a clear indication that neither of them were doing any work. On the other hand, it was far preferable to the various alternatives. When Rory was not so engaged he would wander around the classroom poking his pen into pupils' faces, pulling their work away from them, scribbling on the desks, bashing on the walls, and generally cussing and swearing.

Having made some headway at last with Year 8, I decided that enough was enough with Year 9. We were studying *Romeo and Juliet*, and the class was generally doing what I wanted. I had written out a worksheet that was fool-proof in every way; it required no upfront teacher explanation, it was relevant to the exam that they had to take in a week's time, it contained good, challenging questions that forced the students to engage with Shakespeare's language. Everyone was writing. Everyone, that is, except Rory and Janice. He was in his normal position, between her breasts, laughing and giggling.

"Could you get on with your work please, Rory?" I asked politely.

"I am working, sir," he said, letting his head rise from her shirt.

"No. You need to sit down on your seat and answer the questions," I said.

"Oh come on sir. We're doing the work," he said.

"You are not," I replied.

"But we are Romeo and Juliet sir," he squeaked.

"No, Rory, you are not Romeo. Janice is not Juliet. Now go and sit in your seat," I said.

After these remarks, Janice started wriggling underneath Rory, trying to get him off her. She said that she wanted to do the work and tried to push her lover boy off her lap. But he clung on as she squirmed around beneath him.

"Get off, Rory! Get off me, you perv! Sir, he's raping me!" she shouted with a big smile on her face.

Rory smirked as he continued to cling on to her. "Do you see that sir? Do you see the way she's wriggling? That's because she's sore! I fucked her so long last night that she's sore! It was Rory's big night last night!"

Their antics were disrupting the whole class now. I got angry. "Rory, get out now!" I shouted. "Out! Out!"

In a way, I had over reacted but I was desperate. I felt that my hardwon new authority might vanish into the air if I didn't admonish Rory for his 'big night' comment. He had to go. I had to remove him from the class so that I could restore calm.

He did leave the classroom because Janice pushed him off her. But once outside he caused trouble by begging to come in again, pulling faces at the door, and banging on the walls.

My lesson was ruined. No one returned to their work. Everyone was talking about Rory's big night. He must have been lying, but a lot of the kids seemed to believe him. They were genuinely impressed by his sexual prowess. I wanted to scream out that he was lying through his teeth and that they should ignore the stupid, squeaky twerp and get on with their work, but I didn't. I returned to my desk and slumped down into my seat. Unfortunately, some fucker had placed a whole load of pins and staples there and they seared into my behind. I punched the desk in frustration, but no one noticed. It was no good. It was pointless even trying to find out who had done it. I moved my stinging bottom to a plastic chair, and gazed forlornly at my watch. Jesus, I had aeons to go. Fifteen minutes. Noise and chaos reigned as I nursed my backside in a state of numbed exhaustion.

TIN-CANNING THE SCHOOL VAN

I suppose that the disaster of this lesson might account for the fact that I was not in a great mood that lunch-time when Roger Smith showed me how to drive the minibus in the school car park. In the far reaches of my mind, I could hear him saying that I should make sure that I turned round the corners at a real distance.

"Remember that mate. Be real careful driving around the corners. This van ain't a car. It needs room. Plenty of room," he said, fixing me with his eyes, and gesturing with his hands.

But I was miles and miles away – still trying to figure out how to deal with Rory. Why did Janice go along with him? It was inexplicable and extremely annoying. I determined that I would have to report him to the Deputy Head for his behaviour.

I was still distracted when I escorted my sixth form class into the van. The class, who were normally very well behaved, were extremely excited about going to the gallery. They piled into the van, shouting about where they were going. Apparently, Pullum hadn't told them, and my brain was sufficiently scrambled that I didn't explain either. Confusion reigned as they joshed and bashed each other in the back of the van.

I put on my safety belt, started up the van and drove to the school gates. As the thick iron bars of the gate rose into view, they looked very narrow, and the minibus suddenly felt very wide. I tried to manoeuvre it through. There was a loud, shuddering, scraping sound as a railing that protruded some way from the gate sliced into the side of the van.

The kids started screaming for me to stop, but something impelled me to go on and get out of the gates. Whatever happened I was determined to get the hell out of the school. Once in the road, I jumped out and saw what had happened. The railing had cut open the side of the van leaving a large horizontal scar along the length of it, just where Brokers' Academy was painted on it.

I hurriedly reported the incident to Pullum who was in the Resources room. He turned pale when I explained what had happened, but urged me to go with the trip. He said, with an ashen face, that it would probably be fine because the school's insurance would pay. So I drove on, and managed to reach the exhibition without further mishap.

As we gazed at the monumental, transcendent landscapes of Turner, Constable and Casper David Friedrich, my mind buzzed with worries. Would the insurance pay? Would I be known as an incompetent bungler forever more? Should I really report Rory in that case? Or had I stepped so far into all this bungling, that returning would be as tedious as going o'er, as Macbeth once put it?

NOT THE FIRST PLONKER

When I came into school the next day, Pullum cornered me in the staffroom. He had this habit of getting you positioned for his one-to-ones, where no one else could hear what you were saying. To make double sure that we weren't heard, he virtually pressed himself against me, and whispered in my ear in a desperate and urgent way. It felt like we were talking underneath a blanket.

"The PE department are very angry about the van, Francis. It's their minibus. They're not happy at all," he hissed. "Apparently, they're only insured for their own departmental members. Roger has said that the English department is going to have to pay for the damage. It could run into thousands of pounds."

"Oh dear," I gulped.

"And the thing is, I'm afraid I can't take responsibility for this, Francis. It was your decision to take it out, knowing that you had no previous training or experience driving the van. You should have taken a test before you went. That was your responsibility."

"What are you saying? That I'm responsible?" I said, feeling my head swim. The thought of dealing with this on top of everything else made me giddy.

"Of course, you are. Of course, you are. Look, we'll talk

about this later," Pullum said, getting up and striding out of the staffroom. He had stopped short of saying that I had to pay for the damage but he was getting close. Luckily for me, I saw Roger Smith, the Head of PE, just as I was walking to my first lesson. He was a classic PE teacher. A rotund man who spent all day in tracksuit bottoms and golfing shirt. He loved playing little practical jokes. He winked at me.

"I really put the shits up Pullum, didn't I mate?" he said, slapping me on the back. "Best thing you ever did, tin-canning that van. I've been waiting for this moment for years. He doesn't know what's hit him. He thinks that the English department has got to pay £5000 towards the costs of the minibus! I spent all last night faking an invoice. It's great! You don't know how happy this makes me!"

I explained that I had just got an earful from Pullum.

He clapped his hands together. "Pullum's shit scared, ain't he? Now, not a word to anyone, heh? I want to keep this one running for a few days yet."

"So I've got nothing to worry about?" I asked tentatively.

"Course not! You don't think you're the first plonker to do that on those fucking gates do you?"

MR BEAN CONTINUES BEING A PLONKER

Roger Smith's words should have heartened me. They should

have made me see that I wasn't the only one who struggled with Pullum and the department, but I was feeling too demoralised to be cheered up. I winced. I felt as though I was going to cry. I decided my only option was to retire to the toilet where I could sit in peace. I also needed to wee pretty badly: my bladder had been playing up recently. The doctor had found nothing wrong except a nervous disposition.

Brokers' wasn't a friendly place for teachers to go to the toilet. Nearly all of the staff toilets were situated right next to the main thoroughfare of the school. Loud farts, plops, squelches and sonorous pisses could be heard quite easily through the thin wooden doors. For this reason, I liked to sneak upstairs to the secretaries' loo which was well away from the prying ears of pupils.

Today, I rushed up there, desperate to plonk myself down on the toilet, and to lean my face against the white wall and feel its soothing coolness. Unfortunately in my zest to reach this private paradise I pushed violently against the door and found to my horror that I was staring at Myfanwy.

I was horror-stricken. Not only had my lavatory utopia been usurped, but I had managed to humiliate the very person who I really, really didn't want to hate me. I screamed out my apologies as Myfanwy wordlessly, but wildly, slammed the door shut.

My mind raced through the causes behind this latest

escapade. Had there been an engaged sign on the toilet door? The lock had looked as though it said "Vacant" but I had to confess that the lozenge lock had been slightly pushed over to one side. Had it been mid-way between "Vacant" and "Engaged"? Was Myfanwy's negligence to blame or my oafishness?

Did it really matter?

With my face burning, I descended the stairs and, in a state of utter defeat, locked myself into one of the toilets along the main thoroughfare. I sat down and just let my misery stream out.

Weirdly enough, my tears soon turned to laughter. Through my salty eyes, I started to chuckle. The chuckle turned into a roar, and quite quickly I was in hysterics. Everything seemed utterly absurd. What a ridiculous person I was! What a total and unspeakable plonker I was! Had any teacher ever been so clumsy? After laughing at myself, I began to laugh at the school and the education system itself. Wasn't it all the funniest thing? Locking children in a room with one adult and expecting them to sit still for hours on end and listen to the most boring rubbish that had ever been dredged up from some silly twat's brain. (Well, that was my thinking at the time.)

Bizarrely, I walked to my next lesson really uplifted. I was living in an absurd universe where nothing mattered. There was no meaning to anything. League tables, marking books, taking a register, keeping order, writing, reading, thinking. None of it mattered in the slightest.

We were all putting ourselves through this mental torture, and for what? We would all die at the end of it. We weren't going to receive any teaching awards on our death beds.

I smiled an absurd smile at my Year 8 class. John Keats gazed up at me. He'd just managed to knock little Gabriel Tonks off his seat so that he could be closest to me.

"Hey sir, I mean I don't mean to be rude or anything sir, but you look like you've been mugged," he said. "Did someone hit you on the head or anything?"

"I hope you whacked him one," Gabriel Tonks added.

"Go on, sir, mash him up!"

"Did you give him a right hook, and then shimmy to the left, and duck, whirl round like a butterfly, and boof! Got him!" John Keats was lightly boxing Gabriel as he said this. Any excuse for a scrap.

Being slightly out of it, I started to recollect an incident that had happened a week before. It had been relatively traumatic. Perhaps it also accounted for my weird mood.

"You know I was nearly mugged a few days ago. I was crossing the road and this car went through a red light, nearly knocking me over. So I shouted at him, 'Fuck off you bastard, you nearly killed me!'"

Now I really had the class's attention. John Keats was beside himself with joy. He jumped up and down. "Sir, they weren't listening. Say it again. Tell them again."

I repeated my beginning, complete with the requisite swear words – an unusual event in itself because I never swore in the classroom except in my head. My recollection of the mugging incident had occurred because I was feeling so dazed. But as I continued telling the story I realised that I was probably giving them my best lesson. This was real teaching. Talking about the real world.[21]

"So the car stopped, and the driver got out. His eyes were popping out of his head. He was very, very angry with me. 'I can fucking well do what the fuck I want!' he yelled at me. I could see he was a bit crazy. He was suffering from road rage or something."

"So what did you do?" John Keats asked gleefully.

"Mash him in head? Kick his nuts?"

I shook my head. "No. I didn't. I just ran. Ran away and he ran after me. I was pretty scared actually. He looked like he might really lay into me. So I dived in a local estate agents. And screamed that there was this madman trying to kill me.

---

[21] Real teaching. Very little of this is allowed to go on at school. Talking about topics like sex, death, money, jealousy, bullying, and depression in an honest and open way is not encouraged. Take sex education. While pupils receive some fairly explicit lessons about sex in Year 9, the topic pretty hastily dropped after that. There is no consistent discussion about the issue. Perhaps this accounts, in part, for the appalling teenage pregnancy rate in the country.

The estate agent looked at me and said, "Well, that isn't anything to do with me. You'd better get out of here unless you want to buy a house." I looked at the window. The mad driver was still waiting for me. Staring at me with bulging eyes. I turned to the gum-chewing salesman and said, "Yeah, I really want to buy a house as well. A nice one. With a garden. And a garage."

"Haven't got any of them." (I was now imitating the wide boy voice of the estate agent.)

"Well, one without a garage then."

"Oh, I've got garages, but I haven't got garages and a garden."

"Well, one with a garden then."

"I thought you asked for a garage."

"I'll have a garage," I said.

"Hey, are you having me on or what? You come in here and say you're being mugged, and then you ask for all this stuff. What kind of money do you make anyway? What do you do?"

"I'm a teacher," I said.

The guy started to laugh. "You're a teacher and you want a house with a garden and a garage. I mean, you probably can't even afford a lamppost in this area. Go on, get out of here!"

Luckily, the nutter had gone. I left without saying anything more and ran to the railway station, being careful to cross the roads when they were absolutely clear.

When I finished, there was a moment of silence, and then a spontaneous round of applause erupted from the class. They liked my imitation of the oafish estate agent. After their clapping, the comments started to roll in: everyone said that I should have fought the mad driver and not been such a wimp.

"Yeah, then where would I be? I'd probably be in the hospital right now instead of telling you this."

Funnily enough, that thought didn't seem too unappealing. If I had been safely ensconced in a hospital bed with a battered face, I wouldn't have walked in on Myfanwy. My initial absurdist-induced euphoria was beginning to die down, and I was starting to feel reality creeping up on me. I asked the class to open their text books. The lesson, whether I liked it or not, had to go on. John Keats' face fell, but he did reach for his text book.

Then I slumped back into my chair and wondered what was happening to my life.

MEET MOTHER

"My Rory ain't done nuffink like this," Mrs Addison said, looking at the letter she had received through the post the day before. In it, the Deputy Headteacher had explained that Rory had used bad language in class, and had caused a disruption when he was sent out, leaving him with no option but to suspend Rory for a day. My complaint to the Deputy had produced results. I had told him everything that had happened. He was a nice, silver-haired man, who looked extremely tired for a lot of the time.

"The fing is, Rory never swears at home," Mrs Addison said, sitting on a sofa with her son in the Deputy Head's office. She was wearing a lot of gold jewellery and make-up. If she hadn't had so much cleavage showing, she might have been dressed up for church: she had a fancy, white hat, a black, silky-looking jacket, and a tight-fitting blouse that did nothing to hide an impressive chest. She was a 'Sarf London' wife par excellence – her husband ran a courier company, and made a packet. Because he was suspended, Rory was in civvies: cleanly pressed jeans and a Chelsea football top. His mother had a tight arm around him. I realized, with a shudder, that Janice was imitating Mrs Addison in the way she held Rory in class. "He never swears. And he doesn't lie. He ain't a liar. And if he says to me, 'Mum I ain't done nuffink', da ya know what, I believe him. And he says, he ain't done nuffink. And I ain't having it go on his record that he done that, when he didn't."

Her nostrils flared angrily at the Deputy Head. He sighed.

"I don't think Mr Gilbert misheard what Rory said," he said.

I nodded my head vigorously.

Rory buried his head in her arm at this point.

"Well, I ain't having it, I'm gonna complain," she said, stroking Rory's head. But her words tailed off as the Deputy Head said nothing. He was used to dealing with bolshy parents. The softly-softly approach was always the best.

"We'll see Rory in school tomorrow, and it won't happen again," he said after a moment.

"It won't happen again cos he never done nuffink," she said, but her tone was less harsh now. The Deputy's refusal to get drawn into a slanging match had deflated her.

"We're agreed that it won't happen again then," he persisted.

There was no reply to this. Mrs Addison pushed Rory off her arm. "Come on, shufty now!" Rory stood up to attention like a well-drilled soldier, and together the pair left the office.

I thanked the Deputy Head for his help and left as well. He didn't want to discuss anything much. I think dealing with such parents bored him now. He'd probably had far too many of them over the years.

QUITTING

Pullum was all that I wanted to be. He talked about syllabi, schemes of study, different approaches to marking pupils' work and strategies for meeting the needs of children, all in his spare time. He lived, breathed and ate education. He was a model

Curriculum Team Leader. All the paperwork was in place, the results were good, and he appeared to care about his staff.

This was what depressed me most of all. Did I really want to be like him? Did I *have* to be like him in order to succeed in education?

At the end of that traumatic week, I went home and sat down in front of the TV. UK Gold were re-running an old episode of *Dr Who* from the 1970s. The Doctor had his sonic screwdriver and could simply zap his enemies with this gadget, and, if necessary, escape into his spaceship, the time-travelling Tardis.

A most peculiar thing happened to me at the end of the show. As I watched the Tardis, the battered, ancient police box, disappear into the ether, I felt a tight lump in my throat. For the second time that day, my eyes filled with tears. I so desperately wanted to be in that Tardis, churning through the galaxies to a different place, a different time-zone.

And then I knew. I wanted out. I had had enough. I'd taught for six years in various comprehensives in London, and now I'd had enough. I needed to do something else. I didn't particularly want to analyse the reasons why. The poor behaviour of some of my classes had something to do withit, but the pressure to deliver decent results and the dispiriting management were also factors. Tin-canning the van and walking in upon Myfanwy also helped. More than this, I was just sick of it. I needed a break. The system had exhausted me.

LOOSE CANNON

Shortly after this, I applied to study journalism at the London College of Printing. I bunked off school for a day to be interviewed and take the entrance test. There were quite a few teachers there, but only a few made it through to the final round: anyone who failed the basic grammar, spelling and general knowledge test was asked to leave at lunch. Luckily, my time at Humbards stood me in good stead. All of Mrs Lee's favourite bug bears came up: split infinitives, apostrophes, subject-verb agreement, double negatives and so on. (My goodness me, she would have made a great sub-editor.)

And so I passed, and got on the three-month course to be a journalist. Luckily, my wife agreed to support me as I tried to find my way in a new career. I was out!

It felt good to cruise into school knowing that I wouldn't have to deal with pupils like Gabriel Tonks until I retired. It felt good to know that I would actually be experiencing a life other than that of school. School! My whole life felt like it had been lived in these grubby, smelly institutions.

The feeling of liberation made me feel reckless. After a long day, having enduring a particularly gruelling Parents' Evening,

I travelled home on the train with Spencer, the English teacher in charge of Key Stage Three, and Utley, a taciturn, cadaverous character, who taught English and PE. We were all bleary-eyed at having to soothe enervated parents, who weren't able to control their children, and yet were incredibly anxious that their little darlings should attain top marks. The name Parents' Evening could have been replaced with the appellation: Therapists' Evening.

"No, Mrs Tonks, your child could do very well if he didn't have the Attention Deficiencies that I have diagnosed... I have no doubt he will become very successful in his chosen career." Etc, etc, etc.

All this molly-coddling pissed me off now, but it was what we had been instructed to do by Pullum. "You should never utter a negative comment about the children during your professional dialogue with your clients' care givers," he had said to us before the parents' evening.

His pathetic verbiage bubbled up in my mind as we jolted in the graffiti-scrawled train towards our beds. I shook my head at the memory of his lame words.

"It's bullshit, everything he says is bullshit. Pullum speaks a load of utter crap. Clients? Our pupils are not clients. We are not shopkeepers or bankers! We're teachers. We should tell them what to do, and they should listen, but do they? Well, they certainly don't in my classes!"

This was the first time I had ever really talked about anything to Spencer. Although I had mentioned in passing to him that I had some "challenging" classes – to use Pullum's lingo – I had never really tackled the root cause of my discontent. It was an unspoken rule that only losers complained about unruly classes.

Spencer tensed up and stared at me with narrowed eyes. "What are you talking about? Where did this all come from?"

I explained that I just hated teaching at the school and that I wanted out completely. I stopped short of confessing that I had got on a journalism course – I had taken an illicit day off to do the interview. Technically, I should have told the school what I was up to and they would have been obliged to give me the day off. I hadn't wanted anyone to know that I was desperate to escape, just in case I didn't get on the course. Now I was truly free, I was savouring the feeling of them not knowing just how free I was.

"I'm fed up with Pullum, that's all. I think he's terrible. He's impossible to talk to about the really important matters. He keeps pretending that everything's brilliant when it isn't. The kids are going up the wall and no one is taking any notice."

The train came to a juddering halt. It was Spencer's stop. He was clearly threatened by what I had said. His lips quivered, "You're a loose cannon Gilbert. I'd watch it if I were you."

DOREEN APPEARS IN MY LESSON

Having discovered that my technique of trying to intimidate the pupils hadn't worked too well, I had become much "softer" in my approach. I turned a blind eye to bad language, or pupils listening to Walkmans, or general inane chit-chat if it wasn't really disrupting the lesson. I noticed that on average, my lessons were no more or less noisy than they had been before. One consequence of not behaving like a prison guard was that pupils, who could drive "stricter" teachers into paroxysms of loathing, now perceived me more as a friend.

One such person was Doreen. She generally behaved very badly in lessons: talking when she wasn't supposed to, never doing any work, cussing other pupils and occasionally staff, not to mention *constantly* playing around with her make-up. Her English teacher, Mrs Jones, couldn't stand her. Doreen was particularly vicious with her: making personal remarks about her appearance and teaching techniques.

At registration, Doreen and Fizzy would sit at the front of my class, frequently complaining about Mrs Jones. "I mean, I ain't being funny or nothing but she ain't gonna be pulling down at Stars wearing them rags," Doreen giggled.

"She makes tramps look good," Fizzy added.

"I'm not sure that you are being very fair on Mrs Jones. You are actually being quite rude," I said, feeling a bit alarmed about the thought of poor Mrs Jones having these two in her class. Mrs Jones always looked harrassed and quiet in school; she wasn't one of Pullum's inner cabal, and didn't seem to have many friends. She was probably having a much worse time than I was.

I caught up with her at break, and asked whether she was having any problems with Doreen. She sucked in her cheeks and exhaled heavily. "That girl is making my life a living nightmare, an absolute nightmare, I can't sleep for thinking about the things she has said to me," she whispered in rapid-fire, anxious tones.

I was taken aback by the force of her words. Here was a woman on the verge of a nervous breakdown if ever I met one. "You could send her out to one of my lessons if you like," I said.

She put her hand on my arm. "Oh are you sure?"

"If you like..." I said tentatively.

A bit later on that day, Doreen stomped into my lesson as I was teaching my bottom set of Year 10s. "That cow, she just sent me out for nuffink," she muttered.

"What happened?" I asked, interrupting my explanation of a short story in order to hear her explanation.

"All I said was, 'I like your dress' and she sent me out." Clearly, Doreen wasn't happy about having to sit in my lesson; she wanted to appear like an adult to me.

"Just sit down Doreen. Do you have any work to get on with?" I asked.

She shook her head.

This wasn't good. My Year 10 class, while not likely to run riot, could be easily distracted. I needed to find Doreen something to do pretty quickly.

I asked her to write about the worst night out she ever had. She thought about this for a moment, and then smiled. "I mean sir, can I swear 'n everything?"

I didn't have time to explain it to her in detail so I just nodded, and scuttled over to a pupil who needed the short story explaining to him yet again. Doreen was quiet for the rest of the lesson. The piece that she produced surprised me.

It read like a weird post-modern text: it was a mixture of poetry, prose, demotic language and various diagrams. It obviously wouldn't suffice as GCSE coursework but it had merit in a peculiar way.

Me and Fizzy get ready in my room
Our hearts are going zoom-zoom-zoom
It's gonna be a great Saturday night out at Stars
We're gonna get pissed down the bars

We put our tans on and then our lipstick
And laugh at all the stupid pricks

We'll see at Stars, but they will buy us drinks
And then we'll be sick in the sink

But it was different this night there was this guy who wouldn't leave
us alone he was well strange he bought us some drinks the music was
too loud to hear him speak he had a beard we laughed at his beard
then he got us outside he said he was gonna do stuff to us fizzy
screamed and she ran away stupid tosser but I ain't frightened of him
so I stay –

She stopped at this point and looked over me. I went over
to her desk to see what she had written.

"What did he do?" I asked.

"Nuffink," Doreen shrugged. "It don't matter. It was nothing. He just talked weird. About how he wanted me to be in
some magazine. You know them kind of magazines?"

"That's terrible," I said, trying to imagine what on earth he
talked to her about.

The rest of the class had caught a whiff of the conversation
now, and were listening intently. Doreen's face lit up. Now she
was playing to a public gallery. "Ya kna them kind of magazines? Them porno mags? Oh come on sir, you must get them
every day," she said, chuckling, her accent thickening into
broad Cockney.

"What?" I was taken aback by this sudden new tack. I had

thought she was going to reveal something to me, but now I was merely the victim of cruel accusations.

"Hands up, youse lot if you think sir gets them kind of mags!" she said, swiveling round to the rest of the class. This was awful. She was completely and utterly destroying my hitherto peaceful lesson.

"Doreen. Stop this. What are you doing? You can't speak like this!" I thundered, going red in the face. The rest of the class all put their hands up and I gritted my teeth. I just needed to keep calm and get this sorted out. It was, after all, just a silly joke. Other kids were calling out now. "Oh come on sir, what do you like the best? *Fiesta* or *Razzle*?"

"I've never even heard of them," I blustered.

"Oh yeah, sure, look sir's going red," Doreen persisted. And then she winked. "It's all right sir, your secret is safe with us."

"Could you please get on with your work?" I said, walking over to a distant corner and refusing to listen to any more comments.

None actually came. The pupils looked at each other for a few minutes, and then returned to answering their comprehension questions on the short story. The sea had got very choppy there at one point, and it had felt like it was going to surge through my weak harbour wall, but suddenly the tide had retreated, and an unearthly peace settled upon the scene. Everyone appeared to have forgotten about the whole thing.

How strange children were! How unknowable groups of human beings are!

Towards the end of the lesson, I tentatively walked over to Doreen's desk who was immersed in more writing. She had stopped describing that night out and was now writing about her mum.

If you looked at my mum first of all, you might think she was a right slag she's all slapped up with slap worse than me 'cos she's a lot more uglier than me she don't have a job at the moment but she used to work for a garage doing the books but she left there 'cos the blokes there was disgusting I mean disgusting they come round, and they got oil all over our sofa one of them did he was a right bastard I told him he should leave he was a Muslim he thought he was God's gift and mum said fuck off to him and then she lost her job.

I wasn't quite sure what to do with this work. It had a raw power to it, but there were no punctuation marks anywhere to be seen, and she still hadn't really grasped Standard English grammar. Where should I begin to criticize the writing without destroying her confidence? I knew her well enough to know that if I did make any criticisms, she wouldn't write anymore. And the main thing was to get her writing.

"This is great," I said. "Can you finish it?"

Doreen beamed. "Do you like it? What grade is it?"

"You'd have to finish it before I could give it a grade."

"What do you reckon: an A or a B grade?" she asked, with real hope in her eyes.

Her work probably wouldn't get more than an E grade.

"It has the potential to be an A grade piece of work, with a bit of work," I said.

Doreen came to quite a few of my lessons after that, and generally worked hard in them on describing her life. There were more incidents in Stars nightclub – getting drunk, having a fight with Fizzy, and another girl – and a bit more about her sad mother who seemed to be living an aimless, difficult life, doing bits of work and suffering at the hands of unpleasant men. Doreen's devotion to her was admirable. She saw herself as a protector, seeing off errant boyfriends, and making dinner for her depressed mother. But, as the months passed, I detected a growing impatience in Doreen. She was beginning to realize that her life might be easier if she didn't have to be "looking after" a mother all the time, I think.

She typed up quite a bit of her work on the computer, and corrected the punctuation errors, as well as improving a bit of the grammar. She achieved a C grade for this part of her coursework but only got a D overall for her GCSE.

In the end, I felt the system had failed her. The GCSE course bored her. There was far too much analytical content that she wasn't interested in, and not enough opportunities for developing her writing and reading skills. If only the course had been better designed, then she might have really learned something at school.

PULLUM DECIDES TO TRY AGAIN

Pullum's smile was hesitant. He cleared his throat as he approached me in my classroom. I leapt up, seeing that it was him. Pullum made me jumpy: did he know what I had said about him? Had Spencer snitched on me? Would Pullum get nasty like he had done with the van debacle?

"Look, Francis, er, I realize that I was a bit harsh with you regarding the stuff about the van. Having investigated the matter thoroughly now, it appears that we are only technically liable for the costs of the van, and that in reality the school's insurance will pay. So we are off the hook! And it certainly is a relief because it has been preying on my mind for the last few weeks," Pullum said, wrinkling his forehead.

He had chalk on his pin-striped suit and looked ruffled and out of sorts. For the first time, I realized that he, too, was a man under severe stress. It was stressful pretending that everything was ticketyboo when it manifestly wasn't, it was aggravating dealing with a department of such differing personalities, and it was positively nerve-wracking affecting the idea that these children were model students. Pullum was probably just as stressed as I was, if not more so.

The students were just about to enter the classroom after the lunch break, and this made Pullum pull himself up. "Look Francis," he spat out. "I know we said at the beginning of the year that you might come on this Arvon writing course in Wales, with the sixth formers, for Activities Week in the last week of the summer term. I know we said that…"

He tailed off. I looked at him glumly. It was the one thing I had been looking forward to: a trip away in the beautiful Welsh countryside learning how to write poetry with the poets Valerie Bloom and Michael Donaghy. I realized now that I was out of the frame: I'd fucked up too much. I had smashed the school van, I'd cocked up my classes, I'd slagged off Pullum behind his back, and – unknown to anyone at the school as yet – I was going to leave the profession.

"You really don't have to take me," I said forlornly.

"Oh no, it's not that at all!" Pullum said. "I was just wanting you to know that I would be the other person going, so that you knew that."

There was an awkward pause as I absorbed this comment. Why was Pullum speaking like this? Was it possible that he was indicating that I might not want to go because he was going on the trip? He didn't have his usual bravado about him at all.

"No. I really want to go. It's about the only thing…" I stopped myself here.

A smile of relief spread across Pullum's features. He clapped his hands together and chuckled. "That is excellent. Wonderful! We can go together. Now, there's just one thing. You will be driving the school van again I'm afraid!"

My eyes popped. They were trusting Mr Bean with the van again? All the way to Wales?

"Roger Smith said that you'd had the best driving lesson imaginable, and that you'd be perfect!"

THE EXTRAORDINARY MICHAEL DONAGHY

Even though he is now dead, Michael Donaghy's features still stare out at me. His peppery white hair, his cherubic, illuminated face – which looked far younger than his forty years – his mischievous, glinting, water-clear eyes are before me again. He is standing in front of a huge, stone mansion festooned with creepers and ivy and looking at me quizzically as I lurch down from the van. Wendy, the person in charge of supervising the school group at the Arvon Centre, rushes out to meet us as Donaghy continues to stare from a distance. The children and I are shattered, having driven for hours and hours from London to this remote part of Wales. One of the other teachers, Dierdre, had arrived a long time before us in her husband's Rover, having taken a few pupils in the big car. I had taken the remaining ten in the van.

A nervy girl, Crystal, hands Wendy a paper bag as she wobbles out of the van. "I was sick, but I didn't know what to do with it," she says. Wendy, obviously a smiley trooper at the best of times, winces and says, "Thank you very much! Thanks!" I can see Donaghy smothering one of his big, cackling laughs from the recesses of the portico. I don't know who he is at this point; he seems very mysterious and mercurial with his black, modish clothes in this remote, mystical place.

Later on, after we have unpacked our bags, and wandered around the amazing grounds of the house, we are properly introduced to our two teachers: Michael Donaghy and Valerie Bloom. They are both important poets: Valerie Bloom played a major role in establishing West Indian poetry as a force in modern British literature, and Donaghy's bizarre, brilliant, metaphysical poems had already made him, with only a few slim volumes to his name, a key name.

His black, drainpipe jeans and black jacket, and quiet American accent, immediately made him interesting to me. He had an ethereal, other-worldly quality which was intriguing. I wanted to be like him: detached but intensely poetic. We spent the evening discussing poets and prosody as we meandered around the grounds and down to the beach. He didn't seem that interested in people as such, only poems. Poems were people to him. He lived with them, he spoke to them. Together he and I explored the recesses and labyrinthine paths of numerous different works. He knew a phenomenal amount off by heart: all of his own poetry, and what seemed to me like the entire back catalogue of Robert Frost. I listened to him enunciate Frost on a twilit beach as we skimmed stones across the sea.

How liberating it felt to be with him! It was the first time since university that I had seriously discussed literature with anyone. I had been teaching English for all these years and I had never come across anyone who just wanted to talk about poetry.

Donaghy was possessed by the theory that the human mind is like a vast palace; that it has its own architecture, that it can be constructed in much the same way as a building, and can be observed in much the same way that great edifices can be viewed. This was why he was so fascinated by memorization: memorizing a poem was a way of constructing the building in your mind. In one of his best poems, *City Of God* from *Errata*, he writes:

He needed a perfect cathedral in his head,
he'd whisper, so that by careful scrutiny
the mind inside the cathedral inside the mind
could find the secret order of the world
and remember every drop on every face
in every summer thunderstorm.

During my walks with Donaghy that week – we traversed beaches, cliff-tops and castles, and perhaps most strikingly the weird toy town, Port Merion, where the cult Sixties show *The Prisoner* was filmed. He showed me the pits of hell: he recited Sylvia Plath's poetry, passages from Milton's *Paradise Lost*, William Blake's lyrics and his own poems. Poems about the terrifying pain of consciousness.

He never really invited me to talk about myself or my own circumstances because he wasn't like that, instead he responded to anything I said with poetry. He turned to me one afternoon, and fixed me with his brilliant eyes as I said that I was finding teaching hellish, and recited this poem, *Becoming Catastrophic*:

Purification itself takes several days. It is agonizing: explosive diarrhea, sweats, retching, shaking, itching, freezing. But by the second morning the flesh turns white and gradually transparent. Fat, hair, and muscle are the last to go, until finally the tough black dots of the pupils wink out and you see through the world's eyes at last...

The sinister, surreal roof-tops of Portmeirion shone beyond the tree shadows in the July sun. He and I looked down upon the bizarre town, absorbing the poem. Yes, I suddenly felt that something positive was gestating from my bleak year at Brokers': it was a purification of sorts.

Donaghy was a brilliant teacher. The class, along with Dierdre and I, would assemble at the vast, wooden kitchen table, clutching our notebooks and sink into the rickety chairs as we waited for Donaghy to appear, like a Bronx-bred Puck, from behind one of the oak columns that propped up the ancient, rolling ceiling.

When he surfaced from the shadows, he would stand still and silent, his eyes gazing into the porticoes of his own mind. He wasn't waiting for silence. He was waiting to open the door to the cathedral and step inside. By then we were all silent.

With sparkling eyes, he would exclaim: "Shut your eyes and think of an object!"

We couldn't do anything but obey. Suddenly, the boisterous sixth formers had all shut their eyes and were meditating.

"Now what does this object smell like? Sniff the air! Linger around the object! Then write down some notes."

Immediately I was back in my grandparents' garden, observing my grandfather's telescope. I wrote: "Fresh silver paint, the stinging night air, the smell of oil."

After he had asked us to read out our answers, he continued:

"What does it sound like?"

I wrote: "The minute clicking of the eye-piece, bring the stars into focus."

His reaction to this line when I read it out was revealing of how Donaghy operated. He was ecstatic. His eyes glowed and he jumped up. "Yes, yes. This is it. This is the way to write: never give the game away too early. Get the reader thinking. Get them to construct the world out of tiny details. Get them to see the thunderstorm by describing the drop. That makes me think about the telescope. I am there with you."

I never received any more praise from him because all the other stuff I wrote was relatively pedestrian. But he managed to extract some pretty amazing pieces from the sixth formers with his probing questions.

"Where does it live?" he would say. "You open a door and surprise it, what is it doing? How did the object become this way?"

Or, trying a different trick, he would say: "I have here in my bag, a number of objects. I want to hand them out secretly to you and get you to describe them in an unusual way. Then we'll see if we can guess what your object is."

And what great objects they were! They were so Michael Donaghy! I was given a tiny harmonica in a crumpled box that was labeled with a sticker that said: "Pee Wee – Made in Occupied Japan". Where on earth had he got that from? Other objects were: a scratched and smashed 45 record; a bell; rosary beads; a box of matches inscribed with the words 'England's Glory'; a melted tape cassette; a love locket on a chain; a key; a compass; and an alarm clock pointing to midnight.

Nearly all of the pieces that were published in the anthology at the end of the week came from these sessions. Re-reading them now, I realize what a fantastic teacher Donaghy was. He produced better work from my English set than I had managed all year. The poem he wrote to his baby son during that week is poignant now:

For Ruairi

You haven't seen me. I didn't say this.
The improbable stars underfoot are aligned
Like night lights left on by your cot to remind you
And spiral you home down the whorls of your fingerprints
Here to the eye of the storm of yourself
Where it's still
Where it's soft
Where it's warm. Rest your head.

And I'll never tell anyone where you are sleeping.
And I won't breathe a word.
And I won't make a sound.
By the sound of this river you'll never remember
You'll sleep in the crook of my heart 'till you wake.

As I drove the pupils back down the motorway, I thought

hard about Donaghy. He was a great teacher. And yet would he have survived as a school teacher? No. Not for one second. He wouldn't have been able to cope with filling in all the silly, turgid reports, or with the amount of marking and preparation involved. And, while he was good at controlling the children for a week, he wouldn't have had the stamina to keep doing it day in day out. He was obsessed by his subject – poetry – and he wanted to impart that enthusiasm to young people. But he was best off doing the odd Arvon course. Real teachers couldn't survive in schools.

Thinking this made me realise I was right to get out. I wanted to be free again. I wanted to be a pupil. I wanted to experiment and think for myself. I wanted to be mercurial and read poetry. Going on the Arvon course only confirmed to me that I was doing the right thing.

THE INTERVIEW

A look of relief spread across Pullum's face when I told him that I was leaving teaching, and going to train to be a journalist. He nodded gravely and said that maybe it was all for the best. I'd noticed that he'd found me a bit of an intimidating presence since we had returned from the Arvon Course. I was confident and iconoclastic now; mouthing my complaints about the school quite openly.

Nevertheless, I sensed Pullum also felt guilty about losing me. He hadn't taken care of me in the way he should have done – I can see that now being a manager myself – and he was anxious to make amends. So much so, that when on the day that he and the Senior Management were interviewing candidates for my job, he came to me and asked who I thought should replace me.

"Look, we're in a real jam here," he said. "We just can't decide between a couple of the candidates. I was wondering what you thought."

By sheer co-incidence I had actually seen one of the candidates teach. I had carried out an observation of her teaching as part of a training course a few years back. I recommended her because she seemed lively and resilient. The resilience would come in handy.

He was very grateful, particularly since it turned out to be the right choice. She became one of his favourites after I left.

LEAVING THE PROFESSION

Although Pullum may have taken the gist of my hints, I never properly told anyone at the school what I *really* thought. In my resignation letter to the Head, I praised everyone, saying that I just wanted to try something else for a while. He wished me luck and said that he thought I would be back fairly soon. He promised to write me a good reference if I ever needed it. He winked at me. Although it was unspoken between us, I sensed he knew the real reasons why I was leaving.

Unlike my leaving day at Humbards, my Brokers' leaving day was quite emotional. I had kept my move a secret until the last few days with the pupils. I was worried that it would lead to a rebellion against me, and all of my demands for work. As is often the custom at the end of term, particularly the Christmas term, the "Video Season" was on: exhausted teachers were giving their voices a rest and letting glamorous Hollywood actors speak above the chatter.

At Humbards, I had had the authority to be completely mean and have the pupils working right until the end of the last lesson, but here, I didn't. I chose a video called *Edward Scissorhands*, which tied in with a unit of work we were doing on fairytales.

My Year 8 class entered the room, sat down and listened to my explanation of why they were watching the film. They were listening now! And I was leaving. Uh-oh, what was I going to say? I had mixed feelings about leaving this class now. I had worked so hard upon them – phoning parents, giving detentions, preparing lessons, marking books – and now they were OK. They were "normal". What was going to happen to the poor sod who took over from me?

"And there is one thing that I would like to say as well. I am actually leaving the school after today. I am going to train to be a journalist."

There wasn't much response from the pupils. They were subdued, tired; it was at the end of term. But after the lesson finished, Gabriel Tonks came up to me as I was unplugging the video and said, "Are you going to be a millionaire now?" This comment took me by surprise. He had referred to me being a millionaire before, but I still couldn't understand where this question was coming from.

"Why?"

"All journalists are millionaires, aren't they?"

John Keats kicked Gabriel. "Don't be stupid. That's the stupidest thing I've ever heard you say since you last opened your mouth."

I explained to Gabriel that I probably wasn't going to be a millionaire. He nodded and added, "At least you won't be a teacher. When I grow up, I'm going to drive a BMW and live in a house."

"You live in a house already," Keats interjected.

"I know," Gabriel said. "But I don't have a BMW."

John Keats was impatient with this conversation, and pushed Gabriel to one side. "It makes me feel stupid just listening to you."

"You shut up you!"

They were about to get into yet another toy fight when I

said, "Gabriel's just trying to be friendly. After all, it is my last day."

The boys stopped fighting and looked a bit lugubrious. They were going to miss baiting me, going to English club, getting their detentions.

"You won't forget us, will you sir?" Keats asked.

"How could I ever do that?"

This cheered Keats up, and he and Gabriel left.

MY LAST EVER TUTORIAL WITH DOREEN

It was my last tutorial with Doreen. As ever – it now seemed like a ritual more established than Holy Communion – she was putting on her make-up with Fizzy.

Although I knew I was going to miss Doreen, my feelings of relief at my imminent escape from the profession were beginning to overwhelm me now. I was feeling light-hearted and frivolous. I only had one more tutor period – lasting ten minutes – and an hour long lesson to endure. Then I would be free!

Feeling exuberant, I snatched Doreen's make-up pack and held it up to my face, pretending to dab make-up on my face.

"Oh sir, whatcha wanna do that for? Ya do know that I'll kill yer if yer touch me PA?"

"PA?"

"Personal Assistant. Me make-up, yer daft bugger!"

She was smiling. I gave it back to her. "Now yer not gonna be naughty like that when youse is a homo?"

"A homo? I'm not going to be a homosexual, I'm gonna be a journalist," I replied with a grin.

"All journalists are homos, ain't they Fizzy?" Doreen said. "We met a few down Stars in the West End. They danced with us, but we didn't have to worry or nuffink, they weren't interested. They was journalists."

I realised that she wasn't joking. Doreen really did think that all journalists were homosexuals. Should I try and correct her of this view?

Suddenly I saw how ridiculous I was being: so what? What did it matter that she thought this? It was kind of funny.

"Actually, I am going to become a homosexual," I said.

Doreen and Fizzy roared with laughter but I kept a straight face.

"Yeah, I'm going to become a homosexual, and then I'll be a proper journalist. It's the only way you can become one."

"I knew it!" Doreen shouted out. "Sir's gay! He's a bendy boy."

She was playing to the crowd now. Most of the class were completely apathetic about me leaving – I hadn't received a single present or card – but they were suddenly interested in me now.

"You really sir? Is this right?" one kid asked.

"Yeah, I told my wife. I said to her, 'I'm sorry, but since the only way to become a journalist is to be gay, I'm going to have to find a bloke.' She was a bit disappointed but she understood," I said.

Doreen was quite concerned now. I had really convinced her. "Maybe youse should stick to teaching?" she said in a low voice.

The bell went and the class disappeared quickly amidst much chatter about my "coming out". But Doreen remained, waving Fizzy out of the door. Once she had checked that no one was looking she reached into her bag and produced a wrapped present.

"You probably should stick to teaching but since yer going I got you this," she said, shoving it towards me. I blinked. I hadn't expected this at all. Her expression of loutish disdain and merriment which she almost always wore before a class full of kids, had gone now and had been replaced by a look of sadness and concern.

I opened the present quickly and saw that it was a Parker Pen. I gulped. This was a big present for Doreen. For all her bluster about going to clubs and so on, I knew she wasn't rich. Many of her stories, I suspected, were made up. I knew from her file that she lived with her mum in a council flat.

"Thanks," I gulped. "This will be useful."

Doreen smiled. "I thought it might be, but you won't turn gay, will you?"

She had dropped her Cockney accent here and asked this in something approximating a middle-class accent.

"You can never tell about these things," I smiled. "But thanks a lot for the present."

With that, she got up and left. And I walked to my last lesson at Brokers, which was disappointingly uneventful. I read a chapter of our class reader with my Year 10 class – which was *Of Mice and Men* – and got them to write a diary entry for one of the characters. Steinbeck's novel never lets a teacher down: I have yet to come across a class who hasn't listened to it, and responded to it with rapt concentration.

I got some expensive presents from the staff; they had put quite a bit of money into the kitty for me. Some of the other teachers spoke affectionately to me.

Perhaps, after all, they were going to miss my subdued, downtrodden air, they were going to miss my Chiapoopoo and "tin-canning" escapades, now the stuff of legend, and they were going to miss me moping around the place like Winnie-the-Pooh – which I learnt, on the last day, had been my nickname amongst the teachers sympathetic to my plight. I left the school clutching a lot of presents, among which was my very own Pooh bear.

FOUR YEARS LATER

I took off my denim jacket, and fanned my face with the newspaper. God, it was hot. The heat seemed to slosh around Whitechapel station like a warm bath in a hot room. There was nowhere to breathe. I had just got back from the London Library where I had been working on a book review for the *New Statesman*. I was now going towards the nursery to pick up my two-year-old son, and then head home for supper.

I was feeling a bit grumpy to be honest; the heat, and the marginal nature of the freelance journalism I was working on, made me feel somewhat dissatisfied with my life. But I was yanked out of my irritation when I heard a loud screeching from the other side of the platform.

"Oi sir! Oi sir! Is the poo poo still driving yer loo loo?"

I looked up and saw a large girl, ten-foot deep in make-up, in a tight-fitting tank-top and what might have been termed a belt covering her lower half: she was waving at me. It was Doreen! I walked over to her platform because she beckoned me with a wave of her arms. I was smiling. I was pleased to see her.

"So come on sir, is it the pooo pooooo driving yer looo looo?" she said, chewing on a gigantic cud of gum, and patting the bench beside her, indicating that I should sit down. She was much more confident than she used to be – I could see that – but more or less the same. Her smile was broad and decisive.

"If you mean whether I'm teaching. Well, yes and no. I've been teaching part time but I've been doing lots of journalism."

"Yer in the media? Yer turned gay then?" She laughed. The intervening years had given her a sense of irony.

"I have a two-year-old son, and a wife," I said.

"So yer really are a journo then, not a homo," she said.

"You could say that. Writing book reviews. Doing the odd interview."

"Yer interviewed anyone from *Big Brother*?"

"No," I admitted.

I gulped. Her question might have seemed a bit crass, but for me it cut to the heart of a problem I was having with being a journalist: even with the so-called upmarket papers, it was the lowest common denominator that sold. Getting contacts with celebrities – no matter how moronic – would get you well-paid work in the field I was in. Book reviewing was at the very bottom of the ladder. Did I really want to be chasing after interviews with the idiots from *Big Brother*?

"I went for an interview for *Big Brother*," said Doreen. "But I turned them down. I met John, though."

"John?"

"Yeah John. The boring git. With glasses."

I nodded, pretending I knew who she was talking about. I asked her what she was up to. She told me quite freely. She had left Brokers' after Year 11, having got a couple of GCSEs, and "worked" in the English tourist resorts of Greece and Spain for a few years, washing up, serving drinks and so on. She had come home when her money had run out to get the money to go back out – to "have a laugh".

"I mean, why stay in this fucking dump when yer can go out to Fally (Faliraki I assumed), and get out of yer head every night? Me and Fizzy, we had the bestest time out there."

"So, you still see Fizzy?"

"Yeah, but I hate her guts. We was gonna get a hairdressers together, but she says she don't wanna now. Fucking minger."

I didn't feel this was a good topic to pursue, so I asked her what she was doing now.

"Gonna get a hairdressers together with Fizzy," she said. "We're both doing a GNVQ in Business Studies, and then we're gonna do it."

As ever, Doreen's conversation didn't make sense to me. But at least it felt true. As I left her, I reflected that there was a degree of sophistication in her attitude. She was pissed off with Fizzy, but she knew that this probably wouldn't stop their dream of setting up a hairdressers together. Or would it? Who could tell? Implicit in her comments was the notion that life is complex; that we live with conflicting emotions about people, about work, about ourselves all the time.

I also thought how I missed getting to know characters like Doreen. Although I was teaching part-time in a nice suburban girls' school, I felt removed from the action. My mind was on other stuff: my book reviews, my interviews, my novel!

It was time to decide what I was – a writer, or a teacher. In the end, I opted to become a full-time teacher again. I joined a new school – a very good state school in Upminster – and within a year of being there I had been promoted to head of English, a job that I was very proud to get. It has been a good decision, but I haven't forgotten what made me want to get out of teaching for ever.

One Monday at the beginning of the summer holidays, I decided for some reason that I needed to go back to Brokers – to confront my memories. With my son, I boarded a train bound for that area. I had spent years avoiding the place because of the anxiety it induced in me. But now I felt more content with my job, with my life in general, I wanted to see it again.

There was no one around because of the holidays except Phil, the site manager, whom I remembered Myfanwy getting in a lather about because of the pictures of the topless girls in his office. He greeted me very warmly. Even though we hadn't seen each other in six years, he remembered me very well.

"Francis old mate, how yer doing?"

I told him a little about my life and then he started chuckling. "Yer know you're still a legend here, don't yer mate? Tin-canning that van! Oh my God, what a laugh that was!"

I laughed weakly. I still felt guilty about that episode. I could remember vividly the fear running through my veins as the gates gouged into the van.

"Look, go around and have a look."

My first stop was the toilets. Ah, how I luxuriated in the fact that I now taught in a school where the toilets are completely hidden away from the pupils! But the school toilets were still there: right next to the main hallway. Oh the agony of having to go for a shit in this school!

And then I visited the Resources Network room. I saw immediately from the notices on the board who was still at the school. Spencer was now Head of Department, and Pullum seemed to have a special advisory role of some sort. Myfanwy was not mentioned anywhere, nor was Mrs Chiapo. The Resources room still had the same air of lugubrious efficiency about it. Jeez, I was glad I had left. No one in the English department really had any fun, except fake fun. Pretend bonhomie. The only people who had a laugh, it seemed, were the site manager, and the PE staff.

I visited my pre-fab, which had been converted into a sixth

form common room. Thank goodness, I wasn't teaching in this horrible room anymore.

I ran down the hill with my son, shouting a cheery goodbye to Phil. We were happy. It was the holidays.

Acknowledgements
Special thanks to Robyn Adams, Aurea Carpenter, Emily Fox,
Rebecca Nicolson, Alex Wade and Erica Wagner for all their
help with the manuscript.

BY THE SAME AUTHOR:

I'm A Teacher
Get Me Out of Here!
Francis Gilbert
1-904977-02-2 PAPERBACK £6.99

At last, here it is. The book that tells you the unvarnished truth about teaching. By turns hilarious, sobering, and downright horrifying, *I'm a Teacher, Get me Out of Here* contains the sort of information that you won't find in any school prospectus, government advert, or Hollywood film.

In this astonishing memoir, Francis Gilbert candidly describes the remarkable way in which he was trained to be a teacher, his terrifying first lesson and his even more frightening experiences in his first job at Truss comprehensive, one of the worst schools in the country.

Follow Gilbert on his rollercoaster journey through the world that is the English education system; encounter thuggish and charming children, terrible and brilliant teachers; learn about the sinister effects of school inspectors and the teacher's disease of 'controloholism'. Spy on what really goes on behind the closed doors of inner-city schools.

"Gilbert is a natural storyteller. I read this in one jaw-dropping gulp."
Tim Brighouse, Commissioner for London Schools, *TES*

The Cruel Mother
A Family Ghost Laid to Rest
Siân Busby
1-904095-06-5   £7.99

In 1919 Siân Busby's great-grandmother, Beth, gave birth to triplets. One of the babies died at birth and eleven days later Beth drowned the surviving twins in a bath of cold water. She was sentenced to an indefinite term of imprisonment at Broadmoor.

The murder and the deep sense of shame it generated obviously affected Beth, her husband and their surviving children to an extraordinary degree, but it also resounded through the lives of her grandchildren and great-grandchildren.

In Siân's case, ill-suppressed knowledge of the event manifested itself in recurring nightmares and contributed towards a prolonged bout of post-natal depression. After the birth of her second son, she decided to investigate the story once and for all and lay to rest the ghosts which have haunted the family for 80 years...

"A gripping tale of madness and infanticide during the Great War... Powerful and disturbing"
Margaret Forster

How to be a Bad Birdwatcher
To the greater glory of life
Simon Barnes
1-904977-05-7 Paperback   £7.99

Look out of the window.
See a bird.
Enjoy it.
Congratulations. You are now a bad birdwatcher.

Anyone who has ever gazed up at the sky or stared out of the window knows something about birds. In this funny, inspiring, eye-opening book, Simon Barnes paints a riveting picture of how bird-watching has framed his life and can help us all to a better understanding of our place on this planet.

How to be a bad birdwatcher shows why birdwatching is not the preserve of twitchers, but one of the simplest, cheapest and most rewarding pastimes around.

"A delightful ode to the wild world outside
the kitchen window"
Daily Telegraph

In case of difficulty in purchasing any Short Books
title through normal channels, please contact
BOOKPOST Tel: 01624 836000
Fax: 01624 837033
email: bookshop@enterprise.net
www.bookpost.co.uk
Please quote ref. 'Short Books'

AUTHOR BIOGRAPHY

Francis Gilbert is head of English at a London comprehensive. He lives in East London with his wife and son. He is the author of two other books: I'm a Teacher, Get me Out of Here! (Short Books, 2004) and Yob Nation (Piatkus, 2006)